"[A] piquant debut. . . . Hunt, who has a master's degree in Christian history from Yale Divinity School, demonstrates scholarly expertise on the apocalypse, but ~l   k accessible to the lay reader th   of humor, and casual, conversa   more about biblical propheci   e this informed take."

— *Publishers Weekly*

"Thoughtful, entertaining, carefully researched, and rapturously (sorry) readable, *Unraptured* manages to be both personally edifying and culturally relevant. With some of the most powerful people in the world making decisions based on speculative end-times theology, we need better stories about what it means for God's will to be done on earth as it is in heaven. Zack Hunt is the perfect storyteller for the moment."

— **Rachel Held Evans,** author of *Searching for Sunday* and *Inspired*

"Zack Hunt leads us on a behind-the-scenes tour of the apocalypse industry, with its many failed predictions and false promises. Thankfully, he also leads us back outside, raising significant questions about the Bible's teachings and prophecies. *Unraptured* is an important book that is going to spark some overdue conversations among religious Americans. Read it now so you won't feel, well, left behind!"

— **Jonathan Merritt,** author of *Learning to Speak God from Scratch* and contributor to *The Atlantic*

"Zack Hunt's exploration of evangelical America's obsession with the end times is a wake-up call for believers to break free from their doctrine of rescue and embrace a faith that resists the excuses, limitations, and assumptions that come with bad theology. Hunt's skill as both a writer and a theologian shines in *Unraptured*, an offering that's as important as it is entertaining."

— **Matthew Paul Turner,** author of *When God Made You* and *Our Great Big American God*

"To those unfamiliar with conservative evangelical culture: be prepared to be thoroughly entertained by the idiosyncrasies of this subculture and gain an accessible breakdown of why many obsess over apocalyptic prophecies. To those of us who did grow up in this culture: you will both laugh and cry over our shared shenanigans—blissful catharsis awaits you. Woven through the humor is a poignant faith story and a hopeful retelling of the rapture mythology that is sorely needed for this time."

—Cindy Wang Brandt, author of *Parenting Forward*

"I feel so seen, Zack Hunt—and understood, exposed, challenged, awakened, and invited. Thank you for writing this book. Hopefully everyone who holds it in their hands right now will be as transformed as I was."

—Carlos A. Rodríguez, author of *Drop the Stones* and founder of HappySonship.com

"For almost a decade, I've watched Zack Hunt use wit, humor, and common sense to poke and prod the church toward action. I can't count how many times I slow clapped while reading this book!"

—Jimmy Spencer, founder of Glocal, a social impact marketplace

"This is an apocalypse book, and this is a prophetic book. But this is not an apocalyptic prophecy book, and that's a very, very good thing. Zack Hunt writes with the perfect combination of scholarship, personality, and humor. Set aside your color-coded end-times charts and pick up this book instead."

—Jason Boyett, author of *Pocket Guide to the Apocalypse* and other books

"I've never read a book that's so warm, smart, funny, wise, and relatable to my own fear-filled experiences growing up in evangelical subculture. If I had a DeLorean time machine, I'd ship *Unraptured* back to my younger self, knowing it'd save me from so much of the fear and self-doubt that's still nestled in my chest today. This is an absolute must-read for anyone trying to make sense of end-times theology."

—**Caleb Wilde,** author of *Confessions of a Funeral Director*

"Zack Hunt could have been an honorary general in the tribulation force. Instead, he has vulnerably and humbly shared his journey from an end-times know-it-all to a theology nerd guided by the peaceful kingdom of God. Readers who grew up with the anxiety of the end times will find Hunt a delightful, winsome guide to a book of the Bible that can be perplexing. Never forsaking his Nazarene roots, love for theology, or penchant for a solid punchline, Hunt offers a disarming insider critique of end-times theology by pointing to a more hopeful and indisputably less terrifying explanation of the end times."

—**Ed Cyzewski,** author of *Flee, Be Silent, Pray*

"Zack Hunt has brilliantly put to words the stories of so many of us who grew up in a part of evangelicalism that was obsessed with being ready for the rapture. He has given voice to why many of us have left behind that theology for something more hopeful and biblical. May those who read *Unraptured* be enraptured in God's love, revealed by Revelation's slaughtered Lamb!"

—**Kurt Willems,** lead pastor at Pangea Church and resource curator at TheologyCurator.com

Unraptured

Unraptured

How End Times Theology
Gets It Wrong

Zack Hunt
Foreword by RACHEL HELD EVANS

HERALD
P R E S S

Harrisonburg, Virginia

Herald Press
PO Box 866, Harrisonburg, Virginia 22803
www.HeraldPress.com

Library of Congress Cataloging-in-Publication Data
Names: Hunt, Zack, author.
Title: Unraptured : how end times theology gets it wrong / Zack Hunt.
Description: Harrisonburg : Herald Press, 2019. | Includes bibliographical
    references.
Identifiers: LCCN 2018045972| ISBN 9781513804156 (pbk. : alk. paper) | ISBN
    9781513804163 (hardcover : alk. paper)
Subjects: LCSH: Rapture (Christian eschatology) | Eschatology.
Classification: LCC BT887 .H87 2019 | DDC 236--dc23 LC record available at
https://lccn.loc.gov/2018045972

UNRAPTURED
© 2019 by Herald Press, Harrisonburg, Virginia 22803. 800-245-7894.
All rights reserved.
Library of Congress Control Number: 2018045972
International Standard Book Number: 978-1-5138-0415-6 (paperback);
978-1-5138-0417-0 (ebook); 978-1-5138-0416-3 (hardcover)
Printed in United States of America
Cover and interior design by Reuben Graham

23 22 21 20 19   10 9 8 7 6 5 4 3 2 1

To Kim,
who opened my eyes to a bigger and better world
than I ever could have imagined on my own

Contents

Foreword

It would happen at sunset: of this I felt certain.

My childhood home sat atop one of those little speed bumps of a mountain just outside the city of Birmingham, Alabama. Our front porch offered a premium view of I-59, the Birmingham airport, and, I believed, the impending rapture. I always imagined Jesus appearing in a glorious sky of pink and orange, flanked by a row of angels whose trumpets would herald his arrival so loudly it would shake the ground. My family would dash out of the house to the front porch just in time to see the bodies of all the Christians in Birmingham floating toward the clouds like untethered balloons. Then a flash of light would take us with them to heaven.

It never occurred to me that I might be "left behind"—I was the best Bible memorizer in my Sunday school class, after all. Yet even when I was seven years old, my religious fantasy was always interrupted by the thought of friends, neighbors, and relatives for whom the rapture would, in fact, be very bad news. I felt conflicted about whether I really ought to ask Jesus to hurry up and come back when I didn't actually want him to, and when his return would mean that millions of people around the world would suffer tribulation and I would likely miss field day at school. (Only later did it occur to me that Jesus could not arrive at sunset for everyone. Considering the persecution of Christians in China, it was a little selfish to expect him to show up at 6:30 p.m. Central.)

Most of us who were raised evangelical in America know this story and lived some variation of it. The end times. The rapture. The great tribulation. We anticipated these events the way one anticipates a Beyoncé album drop: with excitement that it could happen at any moment, and a quiet fear that maybe it won't be everything we dreamed it would be.

Over time, many of us came to question the theology behind this story, particularly when the fulfillment of its prophecies requires so much death and destruction. But piecing together a new and better story has proven a challenge. Does rejecting the rapture mean rejecting the second coming of Christ? Are there ways to interpret 1 Thessalonians 4 that don't require complicated prophetic timelines and pilotless airplanes? And should we read Revelation as a predictor of future events or toss it aside as a helplessly inscrutable creative writing project gone wrong?

As it turns out, deconstructing rapture theology is a lot easier than replacing it with something better.

Enter Zack Hunt.

Funny, humble, and one of the smartest people I've ever met, Zack Hunt is the perfect person to guide us through a better story, and the book you hold in your hands does exactly that. What I love about Zack is that the only thing to rival his skill as a storyteller is the wisdom with which he excavates those stories for their most important and transcendent truths. He is one of those rare writers of faith who can stand respectfully and with gratitude within their own tradition (in his case, evangelical and Nazarene) while offering informed critique of its mistakes, foibles, and abuses. Zack never punches down. He is quick to laugh at himself before anyone else. He shows grace to his critics, gratitude for his teachers, and openness to all he has yet to understand. I daresay he meets his own definition of humility—a quality that "recognizes our own limits and ignorance and sees the limits and ignorance of others not as a chance to embarrass them but as an opportunity to show them the same sort of grace and understanding that others have extended to us."

These gifts appear in abundance in the pages ahead, where I guarantee you will learn something new about Christianity, the Bible, end-times theology, and yourself. I laughed out loud in several places and sloppily underlined entire paragraphs. It's nice to know that someone else was as preoccupied with the rapture as I once was. It's even nicer to know that person has managed to keep the faith even after the rapture ceased to be a part of it.

Some of the most powerful people in the world are issuing statements and making decisions based on an end-times theology that hasn't evolved beyond the speculative fiction that informed my childhood fantasies. In these days, we need people like Zack speaking with clarity and conviction about what the Bible really says and what Jesus actually teaches. As the angel in the book of Revelation likes to say, "Let anyone who has an ear listen to what the Spirit is saying."

—*Rachel Held Evans,*
    author of Searching for Sunday *and* Inspired

1

Left Behind

My bedroom was dark, light just barely peeking through the curtains. My adolescent heart began to race, my stomach clinched in ever-tightening knots. Panic was strangling my senses as I rolled out of bed, calling out for my mom, my brother, sister, anybody. But no one answered. The only sound to be heard was the creaking of old wooden floorboards beneath my feet. Stepping cautiously out of my bedroom, I began making my way throughout the house room by room. Slowly at first, one step at a time down the hallway, peering into each room, hoping, praying that somebody—anybody— would be there. With each empty room I picked up my pace, worried that my worst nightmare had finally come true. I was desperate to find anyone at all, even a stranger who had broken into my house to murder me and steal everything I had.

But all I found was emptiness.

And silence.

It had finally happened.

My worst nightmare had come true.

The rapture had occurred and I had been left behind.

Jesus had come to collect his saints, but I had been found wanting; a sinner unworthy to be taken in the twinkling of an eye to heaven with the real Christians. But why? What had I done? I had been so careful not to sin—at least not too much. I didn't smoke. I didn't drink. I didn't do drugs. I wasn't having premarital sex. I never missed church. I only listened to Christian music, and I had, like, every Christian T-shirt ever made. What else did Jesus want from me? What unknown sin had I committed that kept me on earth with the reprobate?

As I raced through my suddenly foggy memory searching for some reason for finding myself on the path to hell, I threw open the back door to get one last look at the sun before beginning my search for a bunker to call home for the next seven years as the tribulation poured out its wrath on left-behind sinners like me. But then I saw him.

The most glorious thing my eyes had ever beheld.

No, not Jesus.

It was my stepdad.

Cutting the grass.

I hadn't been left behind after all! My family was still earthbound and accounted for. My stepdad had been outside, working in the yard. My mom was running errands, my sister was hanging out with friends, my brother was fishing. And I—well, I would have known all this if I hadn't slept in till the crack of noon.

The end-times industrial complex

If that scenario sounds unimaginably bizarre to you, then clearly you didn't grow up in conservative evangelicalism.

Moments like this one are a regular occurrence for countless people who grew up convinced Jesus will return at any moment to whisk faithful Christians away to heaven, leaving behind non-Christians to suffer through a seven-year tribulation in which the Antichrist will rule the world through a one-world government while horrific plagues rain down on those left behind until Jesus returns to enact a thousand-year reign of peace.

Or maybe the thousand years will start and *then* he will return—it depends whom you ask. What is certain is that you don't want to get left behind. And you don't have to be! All you have to do is say the Sinner's Prayer, accept Jesus into your heart as your personal Lord and Savior, and pay careful attention to the signs of the end times that unfold anytime Israel is in the news. Discerning those signs won't necessarily get you past the pearly gates, but it will help you keep on your toes. If you have backslidden a bit, you'll know when you need to get your act together so you won't be left behind.

Thankfully, discerning the signs is easy. There are plenty of televangelists ready to break it all down for you with charts and diagrams and books and videos. Best of all, these guides to the apocalypse can all be yours for a small love offering of only $29.95. Or if you can't wait that long for the mail to arrive, your local Christian bookstore is stocked full of end-times resources. I should know, because I bought most of them in high school.

But I wasn't alone. The Left Behind series of novels has sold more than eighty million copies, but it is far from the only cash cow of the apocalypse.[1] Long before Left Behind authors Jerry Jenkins and Tim LaHaye showed up on the scene, another end-times expert named Hal Lindsey wrote *The Late Great Planet Earth* to nearly the same acclaim—and book sales. Not long after

Lindsey set the world on fire with guarantees of an impending Armageddon, former NASA scientist Edgar Whisenant had his own bestseller: *88 Reasons Why the Rapture Will Be in 1988.* Spoiler alert: the rapture didn't happen in 1988.

If books aren't your thing, folks like San Antonio–based preacher John Hagee are prepared with oversized charts and weekly television programs, in which his church services are transformed into apocalyptic lectures. Or for the younger generation, there's the Third Eagle of the Apocalypse on YouTube, who is more than eager to explain to you the demonic imagery at the Denver International Airport or reveal the secret prophetic symbols in the latest iPhone commercial—that is, if he's not too busy composing an original song on the end times.

And then there's my personal favorite prophet of the end times: Jack Van Impe, who along with his wife, Rexella, produces a weekly faux news show in which he quotes an awe-inspiring number of Bible verses while breaking down news stories, usually connected to Israel, to reveal how they are clear fulfillments of biblical prophecy.

But that's just the tip of the apocalyptic iceberg. There are rapture-themed movies designed to scare you into not being left behind; bumper stickers to warn your fellow drivers that should the rapture occur, your vehicle will be driverless; and rapture pet insurance, which guarantees that a left-behind heathen sinner will take care of your pet when you get zapped to heaven.[2] To be fair, that last one was revealed to be a hoax, but that only means the market is ripe for a new rapture insurance company should you be looking for an investment opportunity.

The point is, the rapture can take over your life if you let it. Plenty of folks are eager for that to happen, because they've got lots of stuff to sell you. Rapture-related businesses may seem like obvious scams, but that's because you're not terrified of being left behind, or worse—and this is the real fear behind it all—going to hell.

I was.

And so are countless other Christians who have been conditioned to believe that if they don't believe all the right things and do all the wrong things and don't say the right prayer, God will torture them with unimaginable horrors for all eternity. That fear drove my faith for years. It sent me running into the warm embrace of end-times theology, which promised to ease my fears with clarity about the ominous future it predicted and a guarantee that I would be rescued from torment to come.

That was how I understood Christianity for much of my life. Even today, long after I lost my faith in the rapture, the fear of being left behind still haunts me. If I find my wife's pajamas on the bed when I didn't know she had to work early that morning, I panic. I know better. I really do. But the rapture is hard to give up.

Why?

Because when your faith is focused on the end of days, they can very easily become a paranoid obsession that takes over your life. Everything I thought about, talked about, and did or didn't do revolved around making sure I wasn't going to be left behind. So when that cornerstone was removed, I was left wondering, what was the point of having faith at all? Why bother being a Christian?

When my faith became unraptured—when I stopped believing that one day other believers and I would disappear in the twinkling of an eye and leave the heathens behind on earth—I had an existential crisis. All I knew was the Christian life, and all I thought the Christian life was about was not being left behind. So without the rapture, who was I? Why did I need to be saved if the point of salvation wasn't all about escaping earth and getting to heaven?

Those questions drive this book, and they are why this book isn't really about the rapture at all. Sure, the word *rapture* is right there in the title, and we will certainly spend a lot of time talking about it. But this book is about what Christianity looks like without the rapture (which doesn't even appear in the Bible—but that's for a later chapter). It's about what Christianity looks like when we stop focusing on trying to escape earth for heaven and start trying to bring heaven to earth.

This book isn't about the end of the world.

It's about the here and now.

It's about what Christianity looks like when salvation isn't something that happens to us in the future but rather something that God does through us in the present.

Branded with hope

When I first got saved, the fear of being left behind and going to hell had yet to take over my life, but not because it didn't have the chance. I was in church before I had my first diaper changed. Okay, maybe it wasn't quite that quick, but that's how the story goes. My preacher grandfather *had* to show me off in church the first chance he got. And he did. I was born on a Tuesday. By that following Sunday, I was in church. I was back in church again for midweek services on Wednesday, then back again Sunday morning, and back yet again Sunday night, wash and repeat every week. Growing up, I was in church almost as often as I was at home.

The first time I got saved I was four years old. Or maybe I was five. Truth be told, I don't remember—not because it wasn't a profound moment in my life, but because when you grow up in conservative evangelicalism, you get saved so many times they all start to run together. The details get blurry.

I'm grateful to say that my first time getting saved wasn't because somebody literally scared the hell out of me. It was because somebody showed me what it means to be loved, what it means to belong, and what it means to be valued and cared for. It was because someone showed me that all that love and belonging and caring came from Jesus.

Her name was Grandma Ruthie, but she wasn't my grandma. She was everybody's grandma, and she had been teaching Sunday school at my church long before I arrived on the scene. She was everything you would expect a Grandma Ruthie to be: kind, loving, welcoming, generous, and diminutive in stature, but no pushover. She was a grandmother straight out of central casting. Outside of my family, she was the first person who really showed me what the love of Jesus looked like and why that Jesus was worth loving back. There wasn't anything dramatic she did for me to show me that love. She didn't donate a kidney or pay for me to go to college. But she was relentlessly kind and welcoming. You knew the moment she smiled at you that you belonged, that she loved and accepted you just as you were. There was no need to try to impress her. Simply existing was enough for Grandma Ruthie to show the kind of unwavering love, kindness, and generosity that only comes from, well, a grandmother.

Her life was an example I'm only now really beginning to appreciate. Don't get me wrong. Like everyone else who ever crossed her path, I've always been thankful for having Grandma Ruthie in my life. But it wasn't until my faith began to mature and I saw how much my fear of hell and the fear of being left behind had shaped my faith that I became truly grateful for a foundation that wasn't built on those things—a foundation that was built on their complete opposite.

That's not to say Grandma Ruthie didn't believe in hell. I'm sure she did. But I can't recall her ever really bringing it up with us. I'm sure she probably mentioned it once or twice, but the good news she preached to us was driven by love, not fear. Her life was animated by a deep, abiding passion for bringing others into the warm embrace of the God she loved. She knew beyond any doubt that God loved her and was literally dying—or had died—for us to love him too.

If my journey of faith had started out differently from that—if I didn't have a memory of something better than the fear of being left behind—I don't know where I would be today. If my first encounter with God was one of abject terror of eternal torment, and if that was the only God I ever met, I probably would have lost my faith long ago, never to find it again. I likely would have decided that this Jesus fellow really wasn't someone worth following. But that foundation of love permanently branded me with hope—hope that, despite the terrifying images of God that I would later encounter and even come to believe in, this was not, in fact, who God really was.

Unrapturing Revelation

Revelation is a favorite book among the end-times crowd. What the multimillion-dollar end-times industrial complex doesn't point out, though, is that Revelation is about foundations as much as it is about the future. Revelation is as much about beginnings as it is about endings. It's about the beginning of a new heaven and a new earth but only because the old order of things has been transformed, not destroyed.

The foundation laid in Genesis doesn't crumble at the end of Revelation. It's restored as the promise of paradise is made real once more. The foundational relationship between creation and Creator that Jesus built upon with his life, death, and resurrection is made complete, as the world God created is turned into the Eden it was always meant to be. We are the ones who took things into our own hands and transformed the paradise of Eden into the hell on earth so many of us experience today. But Revelation tells us to fear not. Where Genesis plants the tree of life, Revelation sees it blossom. Soon and very soon, Revelation promises, we will be invited back to eat from its branches for all eternity.

But Revelation does more than that. It also proclaims that tomorrow is already beginning to dawn today, because the resurrection of Jesus wasn't just a onetime, one-person event. The moment Jesus walked out of the tomb on Easter morning was the dawn of a new era. His resurrection was the firstfruits, or start, of a transformation that extends to all of creation and continues to this day.

That's not just the message of Revelation; it's the good news of the gospel, the very foundation of Christianity. Christianity isn't just about getting saved and going off to heaven. Christianity is about "Thy kingdom come, Thy will be done in earth, as it is in heaven" (Matthew 6:10 KJV). That's what makes the gospel "good news to the poor" (Luke 4:18). It's the promise that God isn't sitting around, waiting for some distant unknowable day in the future to act. God is at work in the world today, making the lives of the least of these better now.

It's so important to rediscover and reclaim the book of Revelation because, ironically, as much as rapture theology has caused us to lose the true message of the gospel, *rightly* understanding the apocalypse can be the very thing that starts to repair the damage done by the rapture. For as we rediscover what it truly means to live in the last days, Revelation reminds us of the true foundation of the Christian faith and the good news that God is already at work in the world making all things new in and through us.

That's not just the story of Revelation; it's the story of the entire Bible. The story of the Bible isn't the story of a God who whisks people away to safety when trials and tribulations are on the horizon. It's the story of a God who became flesh and who walks beside us even through the valley of the shadow of death. God doesn't promise that the walk will be free of pain. But God does promise we will never walk alone. It's a testimony both to God's faithfulness during times of trouble and to the role of God's people as agents of grace in and for the world.

That was the promise I saw embodied in Grandma Ruthie— the love of God incarnated in my life in the present. It was a foundation of love that left the door cracked open just enough for me to one day walk back through and rediscover my first love or, more accurately, the One who first loved me.

Of course, this book wouldn't exist if my faith had stayed that way. My faith would not have needed "unrapturing" had I stayed on the path of love instead of abandoning it out of fear and self-preservation.

So what happened?

Ironically, I forsook my love for Jesus in the same place that taught me that love drives away all fear: church. I don't mean my local church or even my denomination is to blame for this. At least not exclusively. I mean the church universal—from the local church and denomination to parachurch organizations, citywide revivals, Christian media, youth events, church camp, regular old church people, and everything and everyone else in between—became a catalyst for fear and intolerance and legalism in my life.

I know how confusing that might sound to someone outside the church. It would make for a nicer, cleaner narrative if I had one antagonist in my story—if the "bad guy" wasn't also the "good guy." But that's not how my story unfolded. The church that wrapped its arms around me and showed me the love of Jesus? That's the same church that instilled the legalism and fear of hell that drove my faith for so much of my life.

Unrapturing the church

That's what this book is about: complexity, messiness, and how the same source can be molded for good or for bad. I'm not looking to trash the church or Christianity or the tradition that shaped my faith. Yes, there will be critique aplenty in the pages to come. But that's not why this book exists. The bad is there with the good because that's the reality of my faith journey, and maybe of yours too. Breaking away from the traditions we grew up with is hard. There's a lot about them that we love. More importantly, there are a lot of people in those traditions whom we love, even if we no longer see eye to eye with them.

So while I have plenty of not so warm and fuzzy things to say about the faith of my past and the overall state of the church today, *Unraptured* is not part of a master plan of attack to bring Christianity crashing to the ground (as if I had such power to begin with). It's just the complex reality of life if you grew up in and around a certain type of church. Good people can go astray, or be led astray, even in the most noble of pursuits.

Most Christians we clash with aren't altogether bad people. Their lives are fairly normal, and they are frequently kind and compassionate. We would probably think of them as good, decent people were our encounters with them not defined by objectively bad actions and behaviors—racism, bigotry, xenophobia, homophobia, Islamophobia, you name it. Our sisters and brothers in Christ likely don't see how or why what they're doing is wrong or un-Christlike. They may even see their actions as an important part of taking a stand for their faith. What we might describe as hateful they see as loving, because they believe their words or actions will keep people out of hell. Meet them at church, work, or the store and they're nice to be around. They're otherwise good people, but that blind spot is so dark it makes the light in their lives difficult for others to see.

I know.

I was once one of them.

I was one of those Christians you so often hear caricatured on the news: known for who they hate, who they're trying to deny service to, who they're trying to keep out of the country, and what horrible politician they're supporting. They are just as confused and angry with us as we are at them because they think of themselves as good people who are simply being true to their sincerely held religious beliefs.

I was once one of those otherwise good people, and honestly, I wouldn't want to be friends with that version of me either.

So how did I go from Grandma Ruthie to apocalyptic fearmonger?

How did I go from falling in love with Jesus to being terrified he would send me to hell?

And how did a Christian faith founded on the good news of God coming down to earth become an escape plan?

As they say, the road to hell is paved with good intentions.

2

Old-Time Religion

Do you handle snakes?" It was the last question in my very first interview for a full-time job in ministry.

The interview was held in the youth room of Covenant United Methodist Church, a cavernous space overlooking the church's gym. Huddled around a rectangular table that had been hauled up to the youth room just for the occasion were the associate pastor, a parent, a youth worker, a couple of teenagers, and me. My interviewers were all wonderful, welcoming people with whom I would soon get to share several years of my life. But the thing I'll always remember about that first interview is the last question.

"What was that?" I replied.

The parent asked it again. "Is it true that Nazarenes handle snakes?"

There was a moment of silence as the rest of the interview committee leaned in anxiously, waiting to hear my response.

I let them squirm for a bit, and then deadpanned, "Only on the weekends."

Just so we're all on the same page: that was a joke. Thankfully, they recognized it as such, and we all had a good laugh. The tension of the moment gave way to friendship that would last for years to come.

Personally, I hate snakes. I'm sure some Nazarenes have pet snakes at home, but you won't find snake handling happening on a Sunday morning in any Nazarene church anywhere. Nevertheless, it's a question you get a lot when you tell people you belong to a little-known denomination with a funny sounding name. But again—and I can't stress this enough—we don't handle snakes. We don't speak in tongues either, something else outsiders assume we do. Not that I can blame them. The Church of the Nazarene was originally named the Pentecostal Church of the Nazarene, but we changed that not long after our founding to distinguish ourselves from our more charismatic brothers and sisters.

That's not to say the Church of the Nazarene lacks charisma. It has some—or at least it used to. We have people raise their hands during church services and shout "Amen!" most Sunday mornings. I can still remember Sunday services and camp meetings I went to when I was growing up, where some of the older Nazarenes ran the aisles during worship. But it's been a long time since I've seen anyone running the aisles. We still have camp meetings, although they're typically less rustic than they used to be. If you were looking for snakes in the Church of the Nazarene, that would be the place to find them. The old open-air tabernacle at my church district's campground in the woods of Dickson, Tennessee, was known to have snakes drop down from the rafters and into the choir loft during service. Sadly, future generations of Nazarenes won't get to enjoy such a spectacle, as the open-air tabernacle has been replaced with a modern air-conditioned facility.

But holiness, that stalwart of old-time religion and revivals, is still managing to hang around in the Church of the Nazarene. I don't mean that in a negative way, more in the sense that a lot of Nazarenes of my generation don't give holiness the attention that it used to receive in our tradition. Pastors are an exception. When we fill out the annual paperwork for our minister's license, there's a question that reads "How many people have been entirely sanctified under your ministry in the past year?" *Entire sanctification* is our term for holiness. Even as a lifelong Nazarene and ordained elder, I find it to be, at best, a strange question. But among many lay Nazarenes, especially those who might be new to the denomination, holiness doesn't come up as often as it used to.

Entirely sanctified

The old-timers understandably lament the fact that holiness has fallen off the radar in some Nazarene churches. Holiness is why our denomination was created in the first place. The first Nazarenes were largely Methodist preachers who believed that Methodism had lost its zeal for holiness. Holiness doctrine is not exclusive to Methodism, but thanks to its founder John Wesley, it is a distinguishing emphasis in Wesleyan theology and the Methodism he and his brother Charles created.

The basic idea of holiness is that God has called Christians to a life set apart from the ordinary ways of the world and devoted completely and in every way to following Jesus. It's not a bad idea—really, it's just Christianity 101. But over the years, holiness has developed a . . . well . . . not-so-great reputation. If you were to ask someone what they know about holiness, their thoughts would probably land somewhere between "What is that? It sounds weird" and "Isn't that just a bunch of legalism?" To be fair, there's a little bit of truth in both assumptions.

In the early days—and by early days I mean up until the early 1980s, when I was born—being entirely sanctified didn't just mean you didn't lie or steal or cheat or commit other Ten Commandment–style sins. Sanctification also meant you didn't smoke or drink or play cards or dance or go to the movies or wear gold jewelry or pants (if you were a lady) or . . . well, you get the picture. A lot of that legalism has, thankfully, gone the way of New Coke. But a lot of it remains. Nazarenes are still teetotalers, at least officially. Until fairly recently, boys and girls weren't allowed to swim together at church camp. At my Nazarene college we couldn't wear shorts until the afternoon, and never in class. And you're still not likely to find a Nazarene on the dance floor (though that is more likely due to a genetic lack of coordination than any legislated prohibition). Nazarenes are now free to dance, according to our denominational manual. We can also go to movies, play cards, and wear jewelry, and we have finally permitted women to wear pants and everyone to wear shorts on campus before three in the afternoon.

It may sound silly in retrospect, but in the beginning holiness was a very noble, if sometimes misdirected, pursuit. As I said, the emphasis on holiness predates the Church of the Nazarene. Our theology is that of the original Methodist John Wesley, who, during a service at the Aldersgate church in London, heard a reading from Martin Luther's preface to his commentary on the book of Romans and felt his heart "strangely warmed." People got excited about odd things back then. But who can blame them? Netflix was still centuries away. Anyway, with his heart strangely warmed, Wesley sought out to develop a form of Anglicanism—he was a member of the Church of England—that was methodical in its approach to Christian discipleship. He wanted a faith intentional in its discipleship so as to create disciples whose lives were more reflective of Jesus and were purified of all sin.

To be clear, Wesley didn't invent the idea of holiness or entire sanctification. The call to holiness is biblical. From almost the very beginning of the story of the people of God, God has called the people of Israel to "be holy, for I am holy" (Leviticus 11:45). The books of Exodus, Leviticus, and Deuteronomy don't just list random laws to make life for the people of Israel more difficult; they're showing the people of God how to live holy lives. The cry of the prophets is a call to return to the life of holiness that God expected Israel to live out. Jesus picks up on this foundational call to holiness in the Sermon on the Mount, in which he calls his followers to love their enemies so that they will "be perfect, therefore, as your heavenly Father is perfect" (Matthew 5:48). The apostle Paul continues this call to holiness (Romans 12:1; 2 Corinthians 7:1), as do the writer of Hebrews (Hebrews 12:14) and Peter in his first epistle (1 Peter 1:15-16).

Holiness didn't disappear after the early days of the church or remain in hiding until John Wesley came along in the eighteenth century, but Wesley did give holiness its shape as a distinctive doctrine in the modern era of the church, which led his theological heirs—folks like the great nineteenth-century revivalist preacher Phoebe Palmer—to declare it a second work of grace after salvation. The idea was that we are saved but still need to go through the process of purification from the sinful nature we have been saved from. The methods of Methodism were created to help make that process happen.

As the doctrine of entire sanctification developed, crossed the Atlantic, and took hold in the fertile soil of the Third Great Awakening, the fervent atmosphere of the Awakening's revivals transformed what was once seen as a lifelong process that may or may not reach completion in this life into something that could happen to a person, in an instant, down at an altar. All you had to do was say a prayer and in an instant you would be purified from sin. Forever. Again, if you think that's an audacious claim, you're not alone. Many Nazarenes agree.

But not all. Once upon a time, a pastor friend of mine was sitting in his ordination interview when one of the board members asked him, "Are you entirely sanctified?" It's a question every potential Nazarene pastor is asked. As have many in my generation of Nazarenes, my friend replied that he believed he was in the *process* of being entirely sanctified.

That answer satisfied most of the board, but not all. One member spoke up and said, "Well, I still remember the exact day I was entirely sanctified. I was twelve years old. God sanctified me holy and I haven't sinned since." Without skipping a beat, one of the other board members looked over at him and said, "Well, you just did."

Holiness as service to the poor

Holiness wasn't always that wonky, at least not completely. When the Church of the Nazarene first began, it was led by a man named Phineas F. Breese. Breese was the pastor of the appropriately named First Church of the Nazarene in Los Angeles, California, just a stone's throw away from where the famous Azusa Street Revival occurred, giving birth to modern Pentecostalism. The revivalism of the nineteenth and early twentieth centuries certainly shaped Breese and other early Nazarenes, and Breese held fast to certain social rules that today we would probably label as legalism. But Breese's understanding of holiness was very different from the caricature that holiness has become in the eyes of many people today.

For Breese, the church existed for the least of these. For him, the gospel really was good news for the poor, not just an abstract list of doctrines or a magic prayer. Breese believed that holiness was to be lived out through a life of service to the poor, the lost, the least, and the dying. He famously described his vision for the Church of the Nazarene with these words: "Let the Church of the Nazarene be true to its commission; not great and elegant buildings; but to feed the hungry and clothe the naked and wipe away the tears of sorrowing, and gather jewels for His diadem. . . . The gospel comes to a multitude without money and without price, and the poorest of the poor are entitled to a front seat at the Church of the Nazarene."[1]

It is for that reason that I'm still a Nazarene today. I'm not interested in legalism, but the idea that the Christian life should center on caring for the poor and the least of these isn't just something I can get on board with; it's something Jesus himself seemed to think was at the center of both the gospel and salvation itself. If that's holiness, then sign me up.

Be perfect or go to . . .

Unfortunately, Breese's approach to holiness wasn't the only version of entire sanctification I was taught growing up. In fact, as I understood it, holiness was much more about what I *didn't* do than what I actually did do for others. Holiness wasn't something I celebrated for what it could be; it was something I was actually kind of terrified of. I was never explicitly taught that if I wasn't entirely sanctified I would go to hell, but that always seemed to be the message. Not being entirely sanctified felt like being a second-class citizen, an outsider removed from the holy club. In a world where only those on the inside get to go to heaven, the math was easy even for a kid: be perfect or go to hell.

That's what I thought being a Christian meant: being perfect. Or at least trying every day to be perfect. It wasn't an abstract theological concept to me. I took it literally—as in never make a mistake, ever, and if you do, run down to the altar, don't pass go, don't collect $200, and pray for forgiveness as soon as you can, literally. I typically got saved multiple times a year. Once in the summer at church camp, for sure; there was always a Wednesday night youth meeting that would do the trick; a visiting preacher could usually guilt me down to the altar; and if there was one of those big citywide Christian youth events, I was always the first one to the altar. Of the two million or so souls Billy Graham is said to have saved, I probably accounted for about half those professions of faith.[2]

I've also been entirely sanctified quite a few times as well. The first time I ever fretted about it was right before I got baptized. I was in middle school, and the week before I was scheduled to be dunked under water, I had a spiritual panic attack. I wasn't sure whether I should even be allowed to be baptized because I wasn't sure I was entirely sanctified. I talked to one of my youth workers about it, because even though I had said a prayer and asked God to entirely sanctify me, I didn't *feel* entirely sanctified. Thankfully, that youth leader assured me that it was okay to be in the process of sanctification. But when I gave my testimony to the congregation that had gathered in our church's fellowship hall to witness the baptism, I made sure to let everyone know I had asked God to entirely sanctify me. I didn't want anyone being baptized after me to think I had defiled the sacred water.

But it wasn't just baptism I was worried about. From a very young age I carried a deep sense of guilt about everything I did. Once, during elementary school, I accidentally walked out of a craft store with some small toy I had forgotten that I was still holding when my mom rushed us out of the store and on to the next errand. I had a spiritual panic attack before we even stepped off the sidewalk, because I was certain I was heading to jail and from there straight to hell. Thankfully, I was able to turn around, return to the store, and put the toy back on the shelf without being arrested and shipped off to prison.

A few years later I got my first pocketknife. I felt like such a grownup. I loved that thing. But, as every kid does with their first pocketknife, I soon cut myself while trying to whittle a stick into, um, a pointier stick. I still have the scar—both literally and emotionally. I was terrified of my mom taking away my pocketknife, so I lied and said I had cut my thumb on a jagged edge on the bathroom sink. My mom bought it, but my guilt consumed me—so much so that, while staying overnight at my grandmother's house a short time later when my parents were out of town, I woke her up in the middle of the night to confess my sin. My grandma rolled over, confused, and said sleepily, "Okay, whatever"—or whatever the granny equivalent of "Okay, whatever" is. "I'm sure your mother doesn't care," she added, and promptly went back to sleep. But the situation wasn't trivial to me. It was a big deal, dire even. I had sinned. I wasn't holy anymore. I had to confess and re-up on my sanctification or Satan would come looking for me to drag me down into the abyss. So I woke her back up and insisted she tell my mom. I finally wore her down and she agreed.

Cheating in school? Forget about it. I would rat myself out to my teacher if I even accidentally caught a blurred glance at an answer on a neighbor's test—after I already had that answer filled out on my own test. Secular music? No way. That stuff was for heathens. Now, this wasn't a family rule or anything. My mom listened to oldies in the car and loved Motown, but I didn't want to take any chances. So I silently judged her and made sure my own music collection was composed of only godly Christian music. My first album? Steven Curtis Chapman's *Heaven in the Real World*. I loved it. Had every song committed to memory within a week of first popping it into my Sony Discman. But Michael W. Smith's greatest hits collection, *The First Decade*, was the best music in the history of the universe. To me, music didn't get any better than his ode to country preachers, "Kentucky Rose."

Cigarettes and alcohol? Yeah, right. I would verbally accost smokers in public (behind their backs, obviously—I was too much of a coward for direct confrontation). The closest thing to alcohol I got was Martinelli's sparkling apple cider. My Christian friends and I used to get a bottle of that stuff every year for the youth group's annual New Year's Eve party and pretend we were drinking champagne. We were so cool.

Even my clothes had to be holy. If there was a Christianized version of a pop culture icon screen-pressed onto a T-shirt, I had the shirt. I lifeguarded throughout high school, and you best believe I had a "Jesus is my lifeguard" shirt. And "What would Jesus do?" bracelets—what color do you want? I have one in every shade of the rainbow.

I had to have all my bases covered. Entire sanctification meant *entire*, and I didn't want to take the chance that, come judgment day, Jesus would uncover an area of my life that wasn't entirely sanctified and I would be cast out into the darkness. It was probably that scenario, more than anything else, that scared me the most.

Like a lot of other conservative evangelical Christians, I grew up being told that on judgment day, we wouldn't just stand before the pearly gates and be told either "Come on in!" or "See you never, sinner!" No. Instead, Jesus would call each of us up, one by one, in front of all humanity and the heavenly host. He would read out every single sin we had ever committed, and maybe even show them all on a giant video screen so everyone could watch and join the judgmental festivities. Billions upon billions of people would find out that I almost stole a toy from a craft store when I was eight years old. Hell seemed like a trip to Disney World by comparison.

That's not to say hell didn't loom large in my mind too. It did. But my fear of hell didn't come from my parents, or really anybody else in my family. My grandmother was probably the most sanctified among us. She didn't drink or smoke, didn't have pierced ears, and to this day has never even been to a movie theater; but even she never tried to scare me into loving Jesus

My fear of hell came from others, preachers mostly, but concerned old folks at church, televangelists, and Christian media played a big role too. I don't remember the first time I thought about hell, but I'll never forget all the times after that. They happened all the time, but never more vividly than at that most sacred of evangelical childhood church rituals: church camp.

Hearts and farts

When you grow up in a conservative holiness tradition, even children's camp is tinged with a bit of turn-or-burn theology. Not a lot, but nightly sermons reminded us that the alternative to *not* going down to the altar and asking Jesus into our hearts would be, well, not good.

Altar calls were such a regular part of my youth that, like the salvation they offered me, they've become a bit of a blur—except for the altar call at church camp when I was in sixth grade. That one I will never forget. I was sitting in the back row with a friend, and we were laughing hysterically during worship time. The worship songs themselves weren't funny. We had simply taken it on ourselves to change the words "Heart, heart, I've got Jesus in my heart" to "Fart, fart, I've got to fart." It was comedy gold, at least to two eleven-year-olds. Not so much to our camp counselors, who kept telling us to keep quiet and pay attention. And we did, at least on the outside. They couldn't keep us from singing about farts in our head!

Eventually, the music stopped and the speaker took the stage. I don't remember a word he said, but I do remember the overwhelming sense of guilt he laid on me. Or maybe it was the Holy Spirit. The speaker would have said it was the latter; looking back, I'm pretty sure it was just the former, but maybe it was a little bit of both. Either way, I was terrified that my emerging career as the Christian "Weird Al" Yankovic had me in danger of the fires of hell if I didn't rush down to the altar immediately to get saved for the I-don't-know-what time. By that age I had lost track.

I don't know if you've ever gone down for an altar call, at church camp or elsewhere. But there's an unspoken awkwardness about all altar calls, and it has nothing to do with kneeling down in front of a bunch of strangers. It's the matter of when do you leave. Sure, the obvious answer would seem to be whenever the preacher has stopped praying. But if that is the obvious answer to you, then either you have never been to an altar call or you pray a lot longer than I do.

I'm just not a prayer warrior. Never have been. I don't mean I don't pray. I just mean that I have a hard time praying for longer than, say, a minute or two. I get down to the altar, say what needs to be said, and then I'm done. That night at church camp I found myself, as I so often did, stranded at the altar without anything else to pray about. I had gotten saved—again—and in my sixth-grade understanding of altar calls, that was all you went down to the altar to pray about—unless you needed to be healed from something. I was healthy and saved and stuck.

So I started listening to what the preacher was talking about in his prayer. Holiness preachers tend to do that during altar calls—they'll squeeze in a second mini sermon in hopes of either saving a few more souls or covering a few theological points they missed in their sermon. This guy had the nerve to suggest that maybe there was something more to Christianity than just being saved. Maybe being saved was just the beginning, he said; maybe God was calling us to do something more. Maybe God was calling us to devote our entire lives to service in the kingdom of God. Maybe God was even calling some of us to full-time ministry.

Remember why I was down there in the first place: I was terrified I was going to hell for turning a praise and worship chorus into a song about farting. Even though I had just gotten saved—again—I was worried God was still mad and that eternal punishment awaited.

This was it.

Here was my punishment.

God would punish me for singing about farts by calling me to be a pastor.

As an eleven-year-old, I could think of nothing more terrifying than being a senior pastor. Scared out of my mind at the thought of having to wear a suit and tie for the rest of my life, I went into negotiation mode with God. For the first time in my entire life I had something to pray about during the entirety of an altar call. I don't remember the exact details of our negotiation, but I do know it was intense. And I know what we finally settled on. Or at least what I decided we had settled on.

I would devote my life to God somehow—just not as a senior pastor. Oh, and not as a missionary to Africa, because that was just way too far away and did they even have a Chick-fil-A there? I mean, what was I supposed to eat in Africa if there was no Chick-fil-A? So obviously that was a no-go. We—and by *we* I mean *I*—settled on "Okay, I'll do some kind of ministry someday probably, maybe."

That was the cycle of my childhood and teenage years: get saved, sin, go down to an altar, get saved again, rinse and repeat. The fear of going to hell consumed my every waking hour. I didn't care how many times I had to go down to the altar. If it kept me from being poked with a burning pitchfork for all eternity, I would go.

I had given my life over to Jesus out of love, but fear began to drive the relationship: fear of disappointing Jesus, disappointing my parents, getting either one of them angry, going to hell. And eventually, fear of being left behind.

I think that's why I fell so hard for the rapture. It eased my fears. It promised that I wouldn't be left behind to be tortured on earth or sent down to hell to be tortured for eternity. All I had to do was believe.

End-times theology wasn't a radical turn in my spiritual journey. It was the natural evolution of my faith, the only place my faith was headed.

Apocalyptic intoxication

End-times theology is the American Christianity of my youth in a nutshell. It's driven by fear, it's focused on "me" and the goal of personal salvation, and it promises vengeance against our enemies at the end. It's driven by the fear of being left behind at the rapture, fear of what is supposed to happen at the end of time, and ultimately the fear of hell. But it's also about fear of the Other. Anyone who doesn't believe the same way—anyone who isn't a rapture-believing Christian, or doesn't believe in biblical inerrancy, or thinks it took longer than six days to create the world—becomes the enemy, or at least an unwitting agent of the enemy. Salvation comes not just in the form of avoiding hell but also in the form of escape from the worries of this world. The salvation promised by end-times theology also promises the eternal satisfaction of seeing vengeance poured out on one's enemies.

Not all of American Christianity ascribes to the charts, theories, and timelines of end-times theology, but it's shaped by the same impulses. American Christianity has come to be defined by who and what it's against, by legalism and dogmatism that draws lines in the sand and turns unbelievers into enemies. There is a constant sense of persecution and judgment for standing up for "sincerely held beliefs." And because the goal of American Christianity is getting to heaven, all sorts of responsibilities in the here and now can be ignored. After all, why worry about the world now when God is eventually going to start all over anyway?

That was my faith for years: convinced I needed to be perfect, guilty of not being able to achieve perfection, fearful of hell, judgment, and anybody who was different from me. If someone didn't look and think and believe exactly the way I did, that person was an enemy or at least Satan's willing accomplice out to lead me astray; my allies would all look and think and believe the way I did.

End-times theology actually offered a sense of hope and liberation from the fear. Despite being driven by fear itself, it promised me that even if I wasn't perfect, I could follow signs that would keep me from being left behind or going to hell. When I was raptured, I'd be able to watch from heaven while everyone who ever did me wrong got their just due. For someone desperate to be perfect and desperate not to go to hell, the promise of end-times theology was too intoxicating to resist.

3

Late-Night Television

finally had it in my hands. I had waited and searched for what felt like my entire life. At long last, there it was. For the longest time it had seemed like just a rumor—a myth I desperately wanted to believe was real but wasn't, like the Loch Ness monster or an In-N-Out Burger within easy driving distance of my house. But sweet old ladies wouldn't lie to you, right? That's how it began, after all, in my grandmother's living room. It wasn't my grandmother who sparked the dark recesses of my imagination. It was a friend of hers. Who knows what her name was? I sure don't; I was too interested in what she had to say to keep track of the messenger. Let's call her Nancy.

There was, Nancy told me, an actual, real-life, honest-to-God recording of hell.

It had been captured by miners in Siberia or somewhere else in remote, rural Russia. (Russia made perfect sense. I was a child of the Cold War, and I knew full well that everything evil came from Russia. Ronald Reagan had told me so. It made sense that the entrance to hell would be there too.)

The obviously evil Russian miners had dug too greedily and too deep, and for some inexplicable reason, they had been recording their handiwork. Tucked in between the sounds of their massive drills were the screams of the damned. The screams were faint, she said, barely even discernable. But if you were smart and knew what to listen for, Nancy promised, the sound of tortured people could be heard as clear as day.

I couldn't believe it. If it was true, I finally had tangible, indisputable proof that my faith was real. I finally had something to shove in the face of those smug atheists who thought Christianity was just a myth for the ignorant and a crutch for the weak.

In retrospect, I realize that "proof" of hell shouldn't have been quite so exhilarating. I mean, it should have been mind-numbingly terrifying. I was worried enough about hell as an abstract concept; if that recording was what I would hear for all eternity if I wasn't saved and sanctified, sheesh. I should have been scared out of my mind.

But I wasn't. I needed to hear the cries of the damned myself. However, those were the days before the Internet, and I couldn't just google it on my iPhone and listen right away. If I was going to hear the cries of the damned for myself, I would have to hunt for them the old-fashioned way. You might think that wouldn't be hard in a world obsessed with proving its beliefs are true, but you would be wrong. No matter how many stones I turned over, leads I tracked down, or pastors I pestered, the most I could ever uncover was a handful of people who had also heard rumors of the recording's existence. No one had ever heard the actual recording itself.

That recording became my white whale. My Bigfoot. My perfect cheeseburger. It was out there. I just had to find it. It took years and years of searching, but I finally did. I'm just ashamed it took me so long, because the key to finding it was hiding right in front of me in the place where all great things come from: television.

The television in question was an old-school big black box that weighed more than me and was barely able to fit on my dresser. I had bought it myself and I loved it, especially once I got it hooked up to cable. But having a television in the privacy of my own bedroom was my spiritual undoing, as it has been for so many teenage boys. I was soon staying up late at night, turning the volume down so no one could hear, and wasting countless hours watching things I should have been ashamed to be watching.

I'm talking, of course, about late-night televangelists.

Enraptured by the rapture

It was just a bad habit at first. Out of curiosity, I would flip over to the broadcast home of televangelism, TBN, during commercial breaks while I was watching another show, just to see what crazy thing they were trying to get people to send money in for. But the bad habit soon became an addiction as I found myself compelled to argue with the television, correcting the bad theology of televangelists who couldn't hear me and who, even if they could, wouldn't care what I thought. But not every televangelist suffered the wrath of my adolescent theological expertise. In fact, it was that late-night addiction that led to the great love affair of my teenage years. For it was there that I first laid eyes on *Jack Van Impe Presents*.

If you've never heard of Jack or his faux news show, then you're missing out on some truly incredible television. I was enraptured by it (pun very much intended). By their own reckoning, the show was broadcast to 247 countries around the world, a truly impressive number considering that the United Nations recognizes the existence of only 195 countries on Earth.[1] But that wasn't the only impressive thing about the show. Jack Van Impe also claims to have saved at least eight million people—a figure that would dwarf the two million or so estimated to have responded to Billy Graham's preaching.[2]

Each episode of *Jack Van Impe Presents* was essentially the same as the one before it. Jack's wife, the ageless wonder Rexella, would read off various news headlines that were either intentionally provocative or hand-selected as proof of biblical prophecy come to life. In either case, the headlines were always wholly absent of context so that they remained as shocking as possible. Then, as if trying to cosplay the 1950s cliché of a doting housewife who had to get all her information from her husband, Rexella would turn to Jack and breathlessly await his words of wisdom. With his massive grey pompadour, well-tailored suit, and soothing but passionate voice, Jack would break down the prophetic implications of the day's events by quoting enough Scripture to put any Bible quizzer to shame.

Jack laid out, in what seemed like irrefutable logic, how the week's news events clearly portended the imminent rapture and the rise of the Antichrist. Each week he explained in detail how a new prophecy was being fulfilled or how an old prophecy was being fulfilled in a new way. Sometimes the same prophecy would be fulfilled multiple times by different events over the course of several weeks. But no bother. What mattered was that the Bible was coming to life, and Jack was there to explain it to me.

The show would go on like this for half an hour or so, back and forth between Rexella and Jack, until the end, when they would toss things over to the announcer, Chuck, whose deep, booming voice would rouse your spirit and compel you to open your wallet to send them money for whatever "love gift" they were hawking—usually some video that would give you even more insight into the terrifying but prophetically important headlines of the day. All you had to do was dial the 800 number on your screen, pledge a few bucks, and within seven to ten business days the secrets of biblical prophecy would arrive in your mailbox.

You may have wondered if anybody ever calls those 800 numbers on the bottom of the screen. The answer is yes. I sure did. My first call to *Jack Van Impe Presents* was placed in hopes of procuring a free booklet that promised to unlock the mysteries of biblical prophecy. This may come as a shock, but it didn't. It was basically just a generic trifold-brochure rehashing of the main points Jack made every week on his show. But as disappointing as the not-so-prophetic pamphlet was, the next offer more than made up for it. It was the very thing I had waited a lifetime to find: the mythical recording of Russian miners discovering hell in Siberia or wherever. I still didn't care about the details. I just wanted to finally hear it.

Jack was a man ahead of his time. The elusive recording wasn't relegated to the indignity of an outdated cassette tape. No, my friend; everything with Jack was first class, cutting edge. You can do that sort of thing when you have a multimillion-dollar budget courtesy of people on fixed incomes desperate to know if they're going to live long enough to see the second coming.

Not long after I called the show to request my white whale, it arrived in my mailbox. Well, not directly. What arrived was yet another brochure that told me all about the dangers of hell and how not to go there, and inside *that* brochure was a link to a website. The Internet had finally made it into mainstream American life by that point, and some brilliant soul had uploaded my holy grail. I raced to the one computer in my house and turned it on as fast as I could.

And then waited.

And waited.

And waited some more.

It was the late '90s. PCs took forever just to turn on. Some 187 hours later, the computer was finally booted up, and I couldn't open up America Online fast enough. I signed on, and then . . . more waiting, this time accompanied by those strange noises you had to endure from a clunky dial-up modem trying to connect to the Internet. As I waited impatiently for my modem to connect, I said the prayer of every Internet user in the late '90s: "Dear Jesus, I know I let you down by listening to secular music this week, but I promise it's nothing but DC Talk and Carman from here on out if you will just please, please, please make sure that nobody in the house picks up the phone while I'm online and kicks me off the Internet." Seventeen hours later I was finally online. I typed in the web address as fast as my fingers would type.

And then waited some more.

My Internet connection was slow. It took even the smallest of files an eternity to download. I can still remember the agony of the webpage slowly opening, one line of pixels at a time, like some kind of digital water torture. But there it was at last: a bold, shiny icon that read "Click here to listen to hell."

Subtle.

I clicked on it immediately, and slowly but surely, the humble, unadorned media player began to crackle to life. All I could hear at first was the crackle of electronic noise. Eventually the sound changed, and I began to hear the dull rumbling of what I supposed were the miners' drills at work deep beneath the surface of the earth. And then there it was. Faint at first, just as Nancy told me it would be. But it was so faint I wasn't sure I actually heard anything. So I leaned in closer for a better listen, and then . . . it was over.

I immediately hit "play" again, turned the volume all the way up, and put my ear as close to the speaker as the laws of physics would allow. I could definitely hear something that sounded vaguely like voices, and the vaguely sounding voices sounded vaguely like they were groaning in pain. But it might have also been the grinding of industrial gears or the groaning of workers after a long day of work. Looking back, I think it was probably the sound of people groaning in pain—which had been edited together with a bunch of white noise to create a hellish effect that would be embraced without question by suckers like me desperate for proof to shove in the face of evil atheists.

Color-coded guide to the apocalypse

That was the last call I placed to Jack Van Impe, but it wasn't the last call placed on my behalf. My grandmother called the show sometime later, although I wouldn't find out about it until that Christmas, when I opened up her present to me. It was a spectacular gift my mortal teenage eyes were far too unworthy to behold. And yet it was too mesmerizing to look away from even if I couldn't believe it was really mine.

It was the Jack Van Impe Prophecy Bible that I had been lusting after for months, ever since Chuck the announcer revealed its majesty at the end of a show earlier that year. I never thought I would be so lucky as to own something so magnificent. Bound in crimson leather, with pages gilded in 24-karat gold and words translated into the language of our Lord, King James English, the Jack Van Impe Prophecy Bible was my color-coded guide to the apocalypse. Literally. The verses were color coded to highlight and explain the various biblical prophecies hidden within the text. I was in love.

But it was just the beginning of my love affair with all things apocalyptic. I quickly began snatching up the Left Behind novels too, reading them as fast as Jerry Jenkins and Tim LaHaye could write them. For me and many, many others, the Left Behind books were like works of historical fiction, in that they were nothing more than a slightly fictionalized version of the dramatic and often terrifying events foretold in the book of Revelation. The events in the Left Behind series were real life—or would be soon enough; it was only the characters that were made up. I couldn't get enough of them. Every trip to the mall meant a rush to the Christian bookstore to see if the next Left Behind book had come out yet. Any sales clerk who had the audacity to try to tell me they had no idea when the next book was coming out was obviously part of the Antichrist's conspiracy to keep the faithful from knowing the truth.

Then the unthinkable happened. Well, unthinkable to me, because it seemed too good to be true, and as I knew all too well, evil Hollywood was determined to keep the truth of Christianity out of the movie theaters and would never allow something as indisputably truthful as the Left Behind series to be made into a movie and thus proclaim the truth of the rapture to the world. But it happened! Not only did it happen, but the filmmakers got my childhood hero, *Growing Pains* star Kirk Cameron, to play the lead. I got my tickets the moment they went on sale and dragged my friends with me to the theater on opening night. It was everything I ever hoped it would be. Unquestionably on par with *The Godfather*—even though I had never seen *The Godfather*. Still, it was clear to me from the moment I stepped out of the theater that *Left Behind* would become an instant cinematic classic, destined for Oscar glory.

But it wasn't just end-times entertainment I was interested in. The end times were serious business. And not just at the box office. The fate of my soul was at stake. I had a mission: to figure out when Jesus was coming back and let as many people as possible know about it so they wouldn't be left behind and I wouldn't get raptured only to be sent down to hell when Jesus realized I hadn't tried to convert everyone I ever came into contact with.

But first things first. Converts were important, but I had to get myself ready first. I had to make sure I wouldn't be left behind either, and to do that I needed to turn my holiness up to 11.

I was pretty good about saying my bedtime prayers, but I needed to buckle down if I was going to impress the big guy upstairs. I couldn't afford to miss praying a single night, and I sure wasn't going to be one of those lazy Christians who prayed while lying in bed instead of kneeling on the floor the way the Lord intended. But praying just at night wasn't enough. Someone at church had once told me that prayer should be a way of life. With the rapture approaching, I needed to start taking that brilliant insight seriously. And by seriously I mean literally. If I was in the shower, I was praying. Shooting basketball in the backyard? Praying. Riding the bench during a game? Great chance to squeeze in some time with the man upstairs. Walking down the hallway at school? Praying for the salvation of my clearly sinful classmates.

I was a weird kid.

But I'm not finished.

I wanted to make sure to get all the impurities out of my life. Remember: we're talking about sinless perfection here. If I was going to be holy as God is holy, I couldn't allow anything in my life to go unsanctified. My Bible? Started carrying it everywhere. When it began to fall apart, I duct-taped it back together—both as a practical measure and to show everyone around me how often I read it. Music? Again, only Christian music. That's not an exaggeration. My first concert? Clay Crosse. Don't know who that is? Of course you don't. You had better taste in music than I did. Your first concert proba- bly wasn't in a church either. Mine was. What about my first non-church concert? DC Talk's 1996 *Jesus Freak* tour.

But Jesus was coming back soon, so I had to really double down on my holiness. That meant trashing every non-Christian CD I happened to own so I wouldn't be tempted to listen to it. (Well, except for Puff Daddy and the Family. Some things were just too precious to part with.) But I made up for it by sanctifying my car holy. When I got my first car I immediately set all the radio presets to Christian radio stations. Actually, just one: WAY-FM. I made it my preset for every single one of my radio presets lest I be tempted or accidentally tune in to heathen radio and lose some of my holiness. I smiled proudly whenever my friends tried to change the station, only to find the presets entirely sanctified.

This may come as a shock, but I never got a single girl to ever set foot in that car.

It didn't matter, though. I had more important things than girls to worry about. I was about to be raptured. So once I had my personal holiness fully turned up to 11, it was time to turn my attention to everyone else around me. They weren't my friends and family anymore. They were my mission field. And by "mission field," I mean easy targets for harassment. But that's not how I saw it. Most of them may have been Christians already—as a general rule I only associated with Christians, because "Flee from the presence of evil" and whatnot. But their eternal souls were in danger if they didn't discern the signs of the times as I had. So I took it upon myself to educate them every chance I got.

Sometimes that was as simple as offering them a recap of the previous night's broadcast of *Jack Van Impe Presents*. Other times, my missionary work required more in-depth study— like the time I badgered my youth pastor into letting me lead a Bible study on the end times. When he finally relented, I came prepared with more charts, diagrams, and proof texts than had ever before been assembled in one place outside of a John Hagee sermon. (If you don't get that joke, take a second, google "John Hagee chart." Go ahead. I'll wait . . . see what I mean?) I barely took a breath as I rattled off every detail of end-times theology and biblical prophecy I knew. My long-suffering youth pastor gently corrected me when I got a little, let's say, speculative.

I was insufferable.

Dispensationalism

There were no people, places, or moments that were off-limits to my end-times fearmongering. One time the pastor of our church invited the youth group over to his house for a cookout. His house was on a golf course out in the suburbs, and the weather that day was beautiful. We had a great time.

But it was about more than fun and frankfurters for me. Much more. It was my chance to figure out the future and determine my pastor's eschatological bona fides. You see, I was just a young dispensationalist at the time. But like all dispensationalists, I already had all the dispensations figured out. I just needed someone with ecclesiastical authority to confirm my beliefs.

What's a dispensationalist?[3] We'll get to the details later. But long story short, it's someone who believes in end-times theology—and specifically, that history is divided into seven time periods, called dispensations. According to dispensationalists, we live in a holding pattern right before the final dispensation and, with it, the rapture. When exactly that final dispensation will start is a matter of much debate. And it, along with the rest of the timing of the apocalypse, was a debate I needed my pastor to settle for me then and there, once and for all.

I didn't wait long to grill my pastor with questions. Pun once again intended. He was standing at the grill, hot dogs on but still cold, when I approached to find out where he stood on the end of the world. Was he, as my hero Jack Van Impe was, a postmillennialist who believed the second coming would happen after the thousand-year period of peace mentioned in Revelation? Or was he a premillennialist who believed Jesus would return before those thousand years to personally reign over that period of peace? Or worse: Could he be an amillennialist, someone who rejected a literal millennium?

After five minutes or so of breathless lecturing from me on the end times, he smiled, turned over the hot dogs, and said, "I'm a panmillennialist." "A panmillennialist? What's that?" I asked, as my heart began to race at the prospect of some heretofore-unknown-to-me insight on the end times that not even Jack Van Impe knew about. But it was not to be. My pastor just kept smiling and said, "It means I believe everything will pan out in the end."

I was crushed and enraged: crushed that I didn't have the apocalyptic firepower I was hoping for, and furious that my pastor could be so glib about something so serious. I smiled politely and laughed halfheartedly as the rest of the evening faded into a fog of disappointment and frustration. But that was not the end of my obsession with the end times. Far from it. If anything, it served as fuel for the fire that burned within me to know all the secrets of biblical prophecy. If people told me I was wrong, that just made me want to prove *them* wrong. As much as my obsession with the rapture was driven by a fear of hell, it was also driven by a desire to feel smarter than everybody else and to know things I thought only supersmart people like Jack Van Impe could know.

All the right answers

As strange as it might sound, there is a certain elitism to end-times theology. After all, if you know the signs of the times and know when Jesus is going to return or when the rapture is going to happen, people turn to you for answers, just like they turned to Jack. That feeling was intoxicating. I was a nerd, but I didn't love school as much as I loved feeling smart and having others tell me I was smart. That was—and if I'm being completely honest, probably still *is*—part of the reason theology appealed to me. It was, in my mind, the height of intellectual pursuit. I'm not alone in that sort of spiritual navel-gazing. In the Middle Ages, theology was known as the "queen of the sciences." They didn't mean exactly the same thing back then as we do now when we talk about science. They meant it more in the sense of the general pursuit of knowledge rather than in the Neil deGrasse Tyson sense.

Regardless of how it was meant, I believed it. And if theology was the pinnacle of intellectual pursuit, then I wanted to study theology. How did the rapture get mixed into that? Well, if theology in general is the queen of the sciences, then I thought dispensationalism was the king. Not because it possesses the same intellectual rigor of systematic theology, but because it claims to. It has the veneer of sophistication—of complex thought and serious inquiry. Dispensationalism gives its disciples the sense that they are intellectual giants.

Again, I know it all sounds a bit bizarre, but when you're fully immersed in a certain world—trapped in the bubble, as it were—it all makes perfect sense and becomes incredibly intoxicating. You believe that you've stumbled onto secret knowledge that only the wise can comprehend, knowledge that is also the key to eternal life. Isn't that what Revelation is all about? "This calls for wisdom: let anyone with understanding calculate the number of the beast" (Revelation 13:18). I took it as a challenge—a calling, even. Here was a way for me to impress God and the people around me. Here was a way to save my soul. If I had all the right answers and believed all the right things, I could be sure to be one of the first to be raptured.

Also, I liked to argue. And I liked to be right. Those things kind of go together. End-times theology gave me the opportunity to do both at once—or at least the former. End-times theology is a lot like apologetics. Christian apologetics seek to give intellectual justification to the things Christians believe. End-times theology does the same with its various theories on when the rapture is going to happen, who the Antichrist is, when Jesus will return, and so on and so forth.

Although I didn't have the self-awareness to recognize it at the time, end-times theology also appealed to me because it gave me an alternative to sinless perfection but still guaranteed me a ticket to heaven. Don't get me wrong; I still felt compelled to live as sinlessly as possible so I wouldn't be caught dancing with the devil in the pale moonlight when Jesus returned. But end-times theology gave me a safety net—a redundancy plan in the event that I wasn't able to be perfect.

How so? When I was still obsessed with the rapture, my faith was almost purely a faith of ideas. Repentance was part of the equation, and I felt immense pressure to be perfect. But that pressure was more about being a better Christian, getting more jewels in my crown, and living in a better mansion in heaven than it was about being saved. I didn't want to be perfect *just* to avoid hell. I wanted to be perfect to be a better Christian than other Christians so God would love me more. But salvation, the baseline necessary just to get into heaven? All that salvation required was believing the right things. Faith alone, they told me, was all that was necessary to be saved. End-times theology played both cards. It was the right belief system, and believing in it meant I believed what Jesus said was true and thus I would be saved from hell. But if I really understood its secrets, that would mean I was special, set apart by God to know the mysteries of Revelation and the apocalypse.

The end times weren't just about saving my soul. They were about stroking my ego. The book of Revelation is a message of hope and reconciliation for all humankind. I had taken that good news and made it all about me.

4

Catching Cannonballs

Everyone has their sacred space, the place they escape to for peace and solitude, to rest and rejuvenate. Maybe it's a park or the woods, church or the beach. Growing up, mine was the basketball court in my backyard. Not a real basketball court, mind you, just an old goal perched above a patch of driveway that just happened to be something resembling a rectangle. It wasn't much. The backboard was old, slowly rotting wood. The rim was a screwed-on-too-tightly hunk of steel that had no give, so any shot that hit the rim ricocheted off hard and out into oblivion. The net itself was a rusted metal chain. There was no baseline to speak of. Just a low rock wall about two feet high that stood behind the goal post like one of Homer's Sirens beckoning your knees to crash into it. I answered the call. Many, many times. But I loved my backyard basketball court.

It was my sacred space.

Maybe it makes sense then that my sacred space was the place I used to make my boldest pronouncement of the end times. Or maybe not. I was a know-it-all end-times expert. I would have made the same arrogant pronouncement anywhere, but I just happened to be playing basketball that day in my driveway. But the sacredness of that space gave me an added level of confidence that what I was saying wasn't just my opinion; it was coming directly from the mouth of God . . . via Jack Van Impe.

I had a few friends over that day, Pete, Chad, and Brian, and together we were lazily shooting around when, unprompted, I decided to catch them up on the previous evening's edition of *Jack Van Impe Presents*. My teenage friends were not riveted by what a random senior citizen on Christian television had to say about what was going on in Israel. That didn't stop me from telling them. Good friends that they were, they feigned interest as I explained why Jack and I were convinced the rapture was imminent.

"Really?" Pete said.

Absolutely.

"Like how soon?" Brian asked

"Honestly?" I said, hesitating a moment to do the prophetic math in my head. "I would be surprised if we are still here by this weekend."

They just looked at each other and didn't say anything. Had my teenage self even a shred of self-awareness, it would have been obvious to me that they were silently questioning whether they should call a mental health professional and/or why they were ever friends with me in the first place.

Failure to launch

It all seems so crazy now, but back then it was all so clear, at least to me. News was picking up in Israel, according to Jack, and a peace treaty had to be imminent. Work on rebuilding the temple could begin once those evil Muslims realized their apostasy and handed over to Israel the keys to the Temple Mount. We also had what I thought was the perfect candidate for the Antichrist in Hillary Clinton. Or maybe it was the pope? I wasn't picky. Plus, I'd heard on TBN that some group had already remade all the temple vessels from the Old Testament, so they were ready to go when the temple was rebuilt. Surely Jesus had to be coming back soon to rapture his saints into heaven, right?

Well, he didn't.

But you already knew that. You probably also know of dozens of other recent end-times predictions. But those failed predictions are just a drop in the historical bucket of end-times predictions. Predicting the return of Jesus has been something of a professional sport for centuries, and no amount of failed predictions has stopped people from trying to pinpoint the date and time of his return. Declarations by Jesus himself that no one—not even he—can know the day or hour of his return haven't stopped them either (Matthew 24:36).

We often think of predicting the end of all things as being confined to the purview of the eccentric, but there are plenty of otherwise reasonable Christians who have taken up the sport as well. In recent decades, the end times have gone from fringe speculation to a multimillion-dollar industry. A never-ending supply of experts stand ready to not just tell you when Jesus will return, but help you figure it all out yourself by selling you a warehouse full of books and DVDs.

Despite the prolific business and high-profile failures, such as the May 21st folks a few years ago, the end times are still confusing for the uninitiated, not least of all because the theology has its own insider language. But it's an *insider's* insider language. Kind of like the Shriners. They're an insiders' club within the insiders' club of Freemasonry. End-times theology is an insiders' club within the larger insiders' club of Christianity. Its insider language is based on other insider language. If you're standing on the outside—and often even if you're on the inside—it can all be incredibly confusing.

You may already be confused after reading the last chapter, or even that last sentence. I don't want to assume you know all the lingo. And though I don't want to bog you down in a dictionary of words you'll never use in real-life conversations, I also don't want you to have to stop and google every term or, worse, have to ask a family member who *does* know what those terms mean and then get stuck talking to them for hours about how Donald Trump is fulfilling biblical prophecy by moving the U.S. embassy to Jerusalem. (You almost certainly have that family member whether you know it or not.)

So before we go any further, allow me to take you on a brief tour of the apocalypse. Our foray into the apocalypse is not intended to simply bring you up to speed on all the insider lingo. If we're going to understand why end-times theology is both incredibly relevant and incredibly problematic, we first need to understand what is being proclaimed.

Without further ado, here are the answers to all the questions you're too embarrassed to ask or too lazy to google. You need to know these terms before we go any further down the path to the apocalypse. I promise I'll be brief.

Apocalyptic lingo

First up: What exactly is *biblical prophecy* anyway? Now, you might be thinking to yourself, "I'm not *that* dumb. I know

what biblical prophecy is." But you'd probably be wrong
about that. I'm sure you know what biblical prophecy is in
the popular-Left-Behind-Kirk-Cameron-terrible-movie sense.
But one of the most ironic things about biblical prophecy is
that even its adherents fundamentally misunderstand biblical
prophecy. Why? Because biblical prophecy actually has very
little to do with predicting the future.

Of course, you would never guess that from reading the Left
Behind series or watching programs like *Jack Van Impe Presents*. Those authors and presenters would have you believe—as
they themselves believe—that biblical prophecy is essentially a
secret road map to future events. They think the clues to decipher the when, where, and how of those events are scattered
throughout the Bible, just waiting to be deciphered. But that's
not what biblical prophets prophesied about. Actual biblical
prophets—folks like Isaiah, Jeremiah, and Ezekiel—were concerned with calling the people of God to repentance and the
doing of justice. They certainly talked about the future, but to
the extent they warned about future events, it nearly always
involved a scenario like this: "You're acting wicked and unjust
and God says if you don't repent, turn from your wicked ways,
and grant justice to the oppressed, then here's the punishment
that's going to happen."

That's why Jesus can also be considered a prophet, as well
as folks like John the Baptist and even the John who wrote
the book of Revelation. Biblical prophets weren't fortune-
tellers. They were prophetic because they called on the people
of God to repent and demanded justice for the oppressed.
That is exactly what Jesus did throughout his ministry, telling
his followers to "repent, for the kingdom of God has come
near!" (Matthew 4:17) and describing the last judgment as a

moment when entrance into that kingdom will be decided not by doctrinal affirmation but by how we treated the least of these (Matthew 25:31-46).

Speaking of the last book of the Bible: another name for Revelation is the Apocalypse of John. Here again you might be surprised. *Apocalypse* doesn't mean "end times," as so many assume; it means "an unveiling" or "a revealing." Apocalypse *can* refer to an unveiling of the end times, but at the heart of the idea of apocalypse in the Bible is an unveiling of the truth. That truth could be related to present or future events; it's the context that helps us know which. In either instance, apocalypse is fundamentally about truth-telling, not fortune-telling.

Time periods are another biggie in end-times theology. As we already saw in that disastrous cookout with my pastor, another word for end-times theology is *dispensationalism*: the belief that history has been segmented into various time periods, or dispensations. But, once again, exactly what will happen at the end of those dispensations and in what order is a matter of intense debate and has been for a long, long time. At the heart of this debate is the matter of the *millennium*: a thousand-year reign of peace on earth. But that is where things start to get messy. Since the dawn of the church, folks have argued about whether that thousand years is literal or spiritual. There's also a debate about when it will happen. Will it happen *after* the second coming or before the second coming? Also, will Jesus be here on earth to reign during that time, or will he wait to return until after the thousand years of peace are over?

But that's not the only timetable that's up for debate in end-times theology. There's also the matter of the rapture and the tribulation. As we'll see in a moment, the rapture is actually a fairly recent invention. The rapture is the idea that

Jesus will whisk the saints away to heaven in the twinkling of an eye. It's different from the second coming, in which Jesus returns to earth to be with his people rather than taking them away from earth and up into heaven. You can believe in the second coming without having to worry about being left behind, because the rapture and the return of Jesus are two very different events. While this may not initially seem like a big difference—why does it matter whether we go there or Jesus comes here?—the implications play out in rather massive ways, not just in the future but also and especially in the here and now. But I'm getting ahead of myself. We'll come back to those implications later.

When exactly the rapture will occur is yet another matter of great debate in dispensational circles—and not just in the sense of picking an exact date. The debate over the timing of the rapture revolves around whether it will happen before, during, or after the so-called *tribulation*: a period of seven years during which God will supposedly rain down hellfire on those who haven't been raptured—those who have been "left behind." It's during this seven-year tribulation that most of the exciting stuff associated with Revelation and the end times is supposed to occur. This is when the Antichrist is supposed to reign and when the mark of the beast will be stamped on hands or foreheads as a requirement to buy or sell anything (Revelation 13:16-17). This is also the period when all the nasty things from Revelation will happen; I'm talking about the bowls of wrath, the moon turning to blood, locusts, plagues, the four horsemen of the apocalypse—all of it (see Revelation 6:1-8, 12; 8–9; 16). Fun times.

At the center of all this madness—before, during, and after everything unfolds—is the nation of Israel. Israel is the driving force and center of attention for all biblical prophecy. Every single episode of *Jack Van Impe Presents*, every chart John Hagee has ever created, every book that's ever been written about the end times: they all either center on or constantly reference Israel. It's there, specifically in the city of Jerusalem, that the Antichrist is supposed to sign a peace treaty to usher in his one-world government. It is there that the temple will be rebuilt, there that the Antichrist will defile the temple, there that all sorts of plagues will happen, and there that Jesus will return to establish a new heaven, a new earth, and, at its center, a new Jerusalem—or at least so dispensationalism claims.

Opposing Jerusalem is Babylon, the ancient enemy of Israel that plays a prominent role in Revelation as a coded stand-in for Rome. Babylon worked as a stand-in for Rome because, like Rome, Babylon was an ancient enemy that had conquered and oppressed Israel. John was writing under the yoke of the Roman Empire, so to just come out and call Rome the devil and predict its fall would have been, well, not smart. The same goes for calling the Roman emperor the beast. Some theories hold that since Roman letters also had numerical values, 666—the infamous number of the beast—was a reference to the emperor Nero because his Latin-lettered name adds up to 666. Or maybe it was the fifth-century, Rome-sacking Vandal king Gaiseric, whose numbered name comes out to the same sum. You remember him, right? Of course you don't. Nobody does. So maybe the Antichrist is the pope. Which one? Pick one. Or maybe it was Ronald Reagan. Or Barack Obama. Or really whoever you need to help move your prophetic map along; it's dealer's choice.

As overwhelming as all that information might be to wrap your head around, those are just the bullet points of what you need to know going forward. But if you still find yourself feeling confused, know this: you're not alone. Everything I just shared is the dispensationalist perspective. Very little of it is orthodox Christian theology. Why? Because for the entire two thousand years of its existence, the church has argued and debated about what the end of all things will look like. But not as much as you might think. There has also been plenty of debate about the millennium, but the rest of that stuff? It's all pretty new. What makes it all seem so deceptively orthodox—that is to say, a true and essential part of the Christian faith—is the fact that while the rapture and dispensationalism are relatively new inventions, thinking and talking about the "end times" *does* have a long tradition and plays an important role both in the Christian faith and in the Bible.

Scripturally speaking

The end of all things begins in the middle, biblically or dispensationally speaking. Though please don't hear me saying that dispensationalism is synonymous with being biblical. It very much is not. But both share a beginning place for their end-times theology. Although Revelation gets all the end-times press, a book in the middle of the Bible—Daniel—also plays a very important role in end-times theology. That might come as something of a surprise, particularly if all you know about Daniel is that he was tossed into the lions' den for refusing to bow down to an idol of the Babylonian king Nebuchadnezzar.

But the story of Daniel doesn't stop there. Nor does it stop with Shadrach, Meshach, and Abednego in the fiery furnace. After those now famous stories, we encounter several prophecies in the book of Daniel. Daniel was, after all, more than a lion tamer. He was also an apocalyptic prophet, at least in

Christian tradition. It is from the book of Daniel that many
end-times prophecies spring, including purported descriptions
of foreign invaders in the north and potential descriptions
of the Antichrist (although the Antichrist is never actually
mentioned anywhere in Daniel, since Christ didn't appear
until several centuries after the book of Daniel was written).
Most consequential of all is Daniel's description of "seventy
sevens," which were supposed to "put an end to sin, and to
atone for iniquity, to bring in everlasting righteousness, to seal
both vision and prophet, and to anoint a most holy place"
(Daniel 9:24). It is from those "seventy sevens" that the idea
of dispensations is derived. The seventy sevens are treated by
end-times theology as seven different periods of history, or
dispensations. We supposedly live in a holding pattern before
the final week, which is what makes the era we currently live
in "the end times." Now, there is nothing in the text of Daniel
that describes a holding pattern, nor is there anything to support the idea of seven dispensations. Both concepts have been
invented out of whole cloth by dispensationalists because they
give a structure from which to build out their various interpretations of passages in Revelation. Regardless of their origin,
the dispensations are kind of like the contents of Pandora's
box. The box has been opened, and there's no putting the
dispensations back inside—at least not for those who believe
they've uncovered a great biblical secret.

It's when we get to the New Testament that end-times theology really begins to pick up proof-texting steam. The apocalyptic train doesn't wait until Revelation to get going. It starts
right up in the first book of the New Testament, Matthew,
which features what is often described by biblical scholars
as "the Little Apocalypse." The so-called Little Apocalypse is

found in Matthew 24–25 and is delivered by Jesus himself. (Parallels appear in Mark 13 and Luke 21.) It's in the Little Apocalypse that we first learn about the signs of the times and about "wars and rumors of wars" (Matthew 24:6). If you've ever seen the classic Christian rapture scare flick *Thief in the Night*, you'll recognize the source of that imagery in Matthew 24. Although the exact phrase "like a thief in the night" is taken from Paul in 1 Thessalonians 5:2, the idea of Jesus' return being like a "thief in the night" springs from Jesus' description in the Little Apocalypse of Matthew 24 of a home owner being unprepared for a thief to break in during the night. The Little Apocalypse of Matthew is also where we're first introduced to the notion of being left behind, which comes in the context of a short parable from Jesus that describes men in a field and women working. In both cases, one is taken and the other left behind. Curiously, however, the text isn't clear about whether being left behind is a good or bad thing. In this parable, Jesus certainly doesn't mention a rapture up to heaven. In fact, the way Jesus tells it, it's quite possible that one would *want* to be left behind. Much like in a flood, you wouldn't want to be taken away by the floodwaters; you would want to be left behind.

The Little Apocalypse culminates at the end of Matthew 25. This is the only instance in the entire gospel narrative in which Jesus describes exactly what will happen on judgment day. The surprising thing about his description isn't the appearance of farm animals, however, but how the sheep and the goats will be separated. It's not by their confession of faith, their prayers, or affirmation of doctrine that they'll be sorted, but rather by how they did or didn't treat the least of these. If I had been paying more attention to Matthew 25 as a younger lad,

I might have noticed that the goats aren't sent away because of what they did—something imperfect or sinful—but rather because of what they *didn't* do. Matthew 25 offers a stark contrast from the prophecy maps of dispensationalists, to say nothing of the doctrine of salvation by faith alone. But more on that later.

The next heavy end-times hitter in the New Testament is Paul. Although we know him primarily as the missionary who took the gospel to the Gentiles, Paul also wrote letters that are thoroughly apocalyptic. How so? Paul was utterly convinced Jesus' return was imminent. Thus, all his recommendations to the early church on how to live and behave were based on that assumption. We know this is true because Paul predicates many of his instructions, particularly in his first letter to the Corinthians, with language like "in view of the impending crisis," "the appointed time has grown short," and "the present form of this world is passing away" (1 Corinthians 7:26, 29, 31). Paul also describes the faithful being caught up in the air with Jesus "in the twinkling of an eye" (1 Corinthians 15:52), which is often cited as a proof text for the rapture. (For the record: It's not. Paul is talking about the second coming. We know that because Jesus comes down to meet the faithful; he doesn't wait for them to arrive in heaven. Nor does Paul reference any other return. For Paul, Jesus only returns once, and it's not to rapture the church. It's to bring heaven down to earth.)

Along with 1 Corinthians, Paul's second letter to the Thessalonians also plays a significant role in end-times theology. It's here that Paul offers a description of the Antichrist—or as Paul calls him, "the lawless one" who "opposes and exalts himself above every so-called god or object of worship" (2 Thessalonians 2:3-4). This is the figure who, according to

dispensationalism, will rise up in the last days to take control
of the world via a one-world government, desecrate a rebuilt
temple in Jerusalem, and cause all sorts of other apocalyptic
tomfoolery before suffering a mortal wound to the head only
to rise again from the dead, kind of like a bizarro Jesus.

Finally, we come to the big enchilada: the book of Revelation. If the book of Revelation seems weird to you, that's
because it is. Let's not even try to beat around the bush about
it. It's got dragons and dead sheep and talking scrolls, and
it even mentions whores. The shame! Not surprisingly, there
was a lot of debate about Revelation even making it into the
Bible. (Yes, that sort of thing was debated once upon a time.
Contrary to popular fundamentalist belief, the Bible did not
drop from heaven in its present form. There were lots of books
and letters and even other gospels floating around in the early
days of the church that were taken very seriously by many
Christians, but that, for one reason or another, didn't make the
final cut for the New Testament.)

The inclusion of Revelation in the Bible was hotly con-
tested. Even though pastors today like to talk a lot about how
the original audience would have understood the images and
language of the Bible better than we do today, that's not necessarily true for all of Revelation. The churches mentioned in the
first couple of chapters were very real, and the problems and
accolades John describes were also real. Those churches would
certainly have known what John was writing to them. However, we don't know if early readers understood the rest of the
book of Revelation that much better than we do today. Lots of
Christians during the early days of the church dismissed it, just
as lots of Christians do today. Many saw it—and still do—as
a weird, irrelevant book that's impossible to understand and

which has little if any practical value. In fact, in the Eastern Orthodox Church today, Revelation is still omitted from the lectionary rotation. While the rest of the Bible is split up into various readings for each week over the course of three years, no passages from Revelation appear in that rotation.

This is not to say that no one understood or appreciated the book of Revelation. Lots of Christians did. That's why it eventually ended up in the Bible. As mysterious as it is to us today, there were plenty of images in Revelation that would have jumped out more easily to the ancient reader. For example, the average churchgoer in antiquity would not have needed Jack Van Impe to explain to them what Babylon meant. It clearly referred to Rome, because Rome was the only super powerful, Babylon-like oppressor that John could have been referring to in the first century. Any suggestion that it didn't would have sounded as bizarre to them as television commercials sound to my raised-on-Netflix toddlers today.

But the most awkward thing about the apocalypse in the New Testament wasn't the strange imagery of Revelation. It was the fact that Jesus didn't return as quickly as his first followers expected. Most of the early church believed firmly that the return of Jesus was imminent. Like, any-day imminent. Just take a look again at the writings of Paul. He was convinced Jesus was going to return any day now. When it didn't happen, things got . . . awkward. The church was faced with having to reconcile its expectations with reality and how to explain things like Jesus saying "Truly I tell you, this generation will not pass away until all these things have taken place" (Matthew 24:34).

The early church made a significant transition in its understanding of the last days when it began reading books like

Revelation as spiritual promises instead of literal ones. This was particularly true when it came to the belief in the millennium: that literal thousand-year reign of peace on earth. Literal millennialism was a widespread belief throughout the early church until after the pivotal Council of Nicaea in the fourth century, when an influential church father named Jerome began insisting instead that the millennium was a spiritual truth. An even more influential church father, Saint Augustine, shared this spiritual interpretation. Their authority was such that for centuries to follow, belief in the literal millennium effectively went all but extinct.

In the meantime, other important steps in the development of end-times theology were taking place. For example, in their original form, the books of the Bible were written in one continuous unit, meaning there were no chapters or verses. Eventually along came a fellow named Primasius. While he didn't invent chapters and verses as we know them today, he was the first one to chop the book of Revelation up into sections. This became an important foundational breakdown for later dispensationalists, who base a lot of their timetables on when certain chapters and verses in Revelation begin or end.[1]

While the following thousand years or so of Christian theology saw theologians mostly focusing on the spiritual meaning of Revelation, Christian theology also saw a never-ending stream of predictions for when Jesus would return. Interestingly, those early predictions said nothing about the rapture. Why? *Because it hadn't yet been invented.*

One thing the early church would not have recognized in Revelation—or anywhere else in the New Testament—is the rapture. Not because early believers were biblically illiterate, but because it's simply not there. In fact, the rapture didn't appear on the church's radar until the late nineteenth century, when it was invented by an Anglo-Irish preacher by the name of John Nelson Darby.

Inventing the rapture

No one is more important or influential in the history of end-times theology than John Darby. Born in London in 1800, Darby was the forefather of dispensationalism and, in particular, the idea of the rapture. Ordained in the Church of Ireland in 1826, he resigned his position the following year and went on to help found a sect called the Plymouth Brethren. A prolific writer and preacher, as well as a hymn writer, Darby toured extensively throughout his lifetime, traveling across Britain, Europe, and the United States.

It was Darby who effectively invented and popularized the idea of the rapture. He may have initially borrowed the basic idea from a Scottish teenager named Margaret MacDonald who, while attending a healing service in 1830, is reported to have had a vision of a two-stage return of Jesus. Her vision suggested that yes, Jesus would return at the second coming, but that Jesus would have already returned once before that as well.[2] Whether this vision actually occurred is a matter of some dispute, but it is unquestionably Darby who popularized the idea of the rapture, and with it the idea of dispensations. Surprisingly though, Darby himself was careful to never predict a specific date for either the rapture or the second coming.

Darby's idea of the rapture won over many in the United States during his visits to the country between 1859 and 1877. His dispensationalist theology became so popular and so accepted as gospel truth that the popular Scofield Reference Bible modeled itself on Darby's ideas by including dispensational commentary throughout the text.

When you consider the timing of Darby's visit to the United States, it seems less surprising that he found an audience eager to hear what he had to say. Darby arrived at the onset of the bloodiest moment in American history: the Civil War. If ever there was a time of trial and tribulation in the young republic's history—a time that felt like the end of the world to many white American Christians—then surely it was the Civil War, when tens of thousands could die in a single day. The South's surrender at Appomattox brought an end to the Civil War but not to worry and strife. Reconstruction was anything but paradise, especially for African Americans. Darby's promise of liberation from the tribulations of the day must have sounded like incredibly good news to countless souls living during that tumultuous time.

But Darby was not the only one in church history to come up with, shall we say, *creative* approaches to the end times. While Jesus very clearly said, "But about that day and hour no one knows, neither the angels of heaven, nor the Son, but only the Father" (Matthew 24:36), that didn't stop many people from trying to figure it out.

The end is nigh and nigh again and again and again . . .

From the fourth century on, nearly every century saw at least one person predicting the imminent return of Jesus. The number of predictions picked up steam and became a fairly regular thing as time went on, even after a church council in the sixteenth century officially prohibited people from making such predictions.

Most predictions are your pretty standard stuff—eclipses and comets and plagues that seemed like clear signs of the end to people at the time. But there are some fun stories out there too.

In 1525, Thomas Müntzer was so convinced that Jesus' return was imminent *and* that he would be protected from harm as he and his fellow Protestant rebels revolted against their German monarchs that he promised to catch the enemies' cannonballs in the sleeves of his shirt.[3] Things didn't work out quite the way he hoped. His fellow reformer Martin Luther got in on the prediction act in the 16th century. He was not quite as successful in that endeavor as he was in sparking the Protestant Reformation.

Those living in the American colonies finally joined the end-times prediction parade in 1694, when it was foretold that Jesus would return to Pennsylvania. He didn't. At least not that I am aware of. Speaking of America, many Americans thought the Revolutionary War itself was a sign of the times, with the Stamp Act playing the role of the mark of the beast because it forced colonists to purchase and use stamps on newspapers and a host of other documents. Likewise, King George took the stage as the Antichrist because, well, every story needs a good villain.[4]

Another fun prediction occurred in England in 1809 when a famous chicken was said to lay eggs with secret messages written on them—messages foretelling the imminent return of Jesus.[5] Shockingly, it turned out the chicken wasn't actually magical or divine. Its owner was writing the messages on ordinary, non-apocalyptic eggs.

A century later and an ocean away, the Millerites jumped into the second coming guessing game—literally. Some of them were said to have jumped off roofs, believing they would be caught up with Jesus in the twinkling of an eye.[6] Sadly, Jesus did not catch them, but those who survived the jump went on to form the Seventh-day Adventists. Roughly thirty years later, the Jehovah's Witnesses began an epic and seemingly never-ending stream of predictions and revisions about the second coming. Their predictions came with a clever twist: Jesus did return, but his return was invisible, so that's why nobody could see it. Genius.

Fast-forward to 1977, when *Countdown to Rapture* was published. What, according to that book, was the signal for the rapture's imminent occurrence? Killer bees.[7] They may have come, but they didn't bring Jesus with them.

Remember the former NASA scientist who wrote *88 Reasons Why the Rapture Will Be in 1988*? When Jesus didn't oblige, the scientist wrote a follow-up the next year called *The Final Shout: Rapture Report 1989*. There was no *1990 Rapture Report* because, I assume, the publisher realized it was just diminishing returns at that point.

In 1998, someone predicted that Jesus would return on a spaceship.[8] In the early 2000s, *The Bible Code* made its debut on the dispensationalist scene, promising to use computer wizardry to unlock secret codes hidden in the Bible. It didn't. Believe it or not, ancient people who had no concept of computers probably also had no way of imagining codes that only machines—the very existence of which they couldn't imagine—would be able to figure out.

The year 2004 saw another apocalyptic code gain popularity. *The Noah Code* claimed it could predict the second coming by examining the story of Noah. Unfortunately for those who bought the book, it turns out that Noah was better at building boats than predicting the return of Jesus.

In 2012, some folks in the United States made quite the stir when they predicted the rapture would happen on May 21st of that year. They spent countless thousands of dollars buying up billboards and driving vans plastered with rapture warnings across the country to spread the word. They were even kind enough to grant me an interview for my blog.[9] Although nothing I could say caused them to waver in their beliefs, when I asked if they would be open to a follow-up interview if their prediction didn't pan out, they laughingly agreed, saying there was no way they were wrong. When the rapture failed to occur and I requested that follow-up interview, their spokesperson emailed me back to say, "no comment."

But none of those figures, prognosticators, or prophetic models hold a candle to the juggernaut that was the Left Behind series. This blockbuster series of novels and related products didn't offer an exact prediction of a certain date, but it did sell millions of dollars' worth of merchandise. Though classified as fiction, the books were presented as a sort of future history—a creative documentary of what the Bible supposedly says is to come.

What resulted from the Left Behind series, as well as from its predecessors, imitators, and heirs, was a massive end-times racket. While ostensibly explaining the mysteries of Revelation to the masses, the franchise raked in untold millions of dollars in the process. Although Tim LaHaye and Jerry Jenkins are no longer writing more volumes in the Left Behind series, their legacy lives on. The end-times industrial complex continues to churn out new books, new codes, and new predictions, which promise to make sense of the apocalypse—for a price.

So despite all the failed predictions and embarrassing gaffes, why are the end times still so popular? What, exactly, is the appeal of all this apocalyptic weirdness?

The appeal of it all

Looking from the outside in, the appeal of the end times is weird and hard to understand. For many people on the inside, it's pretty weird and hard to understand too. But there's a certain logic to it all. From the inside, dispensationalism seems very rational and almost scientific. To put it crassly, dispensationalism gives its followers the confidence of knowing they're right by suggesting that all the "smart" people are wrong. That can be incredibly empowering. It was for me.

The veneer of scientific or intellectual credibility that dispensationalism offers can't be overstated. Many dispensationalists may not consider themselves intellectuals; they may not even care about engaging in the sort of theological or philosophical debates that academics enjoy. But in the information age, in which everyone seems to be an expert on something, the systems of dispensationalism offer a sense of confidence for those seeking surety in their faith without having to attend seminary or have a working knowledge of biblical languages.

End-times theology also offers a sense of community. This is an often-overlooked aspect of end-times theology but one that we shouldn't miss. Community is, after all, an important element of any faith. Religion gives us a place to belong, a sense that we matter, that we're part of something bigger than ourselves. What could be bigger and more meaningful than the end of the world? For all its gloom and doom and denunciations of unbelievers, end-times theology provides a welcoming community for true believers—one that affirms their beliefs, gives them a role in spreading an important message, and promises a place in the heavenly community for all eternity.

This leads us to a more obvious appeal of the end times: the guarantee that true believers will avoid hell.

The promise that I'd avoid hell—and not just hell but suffering in general, because I wouldn't be left behind to suffer through the tribulation—was certainly appealing to me. The rapture (or at least a pretribulation rapture) guarantees that the faithful will be taken away to the safety and comfort of heaven, where they can watch from the clouds as those left behind suffer unspeakable tribulations. Who wouldn't want to avoid that? Dispensationalism offers you a really easy way to avoid all of it: you just have to believe.

On the flip side of avoiding hell, there's the genuine hope for something better. Yes, end-times theology is full of all kinds of scary plagues, evil monsters, and celestial bodies turning to blood. It's terrifying stuff. But end-times theology also offers a way to escape the danger that is to come. The rapture guarantees that once history is over, true believers will be safe and sound and treated like royalty in heaven for all eternity.

Who wouldn't want to be taken away to heaven? Who wouldn't want to live through a thousand years of peace? Who wouldn't want to be a part of the chosen few? For all its flaws—and they are many—dispensationalism offers something that is universally appealing: the hope for something better.

If you're struggling to pay your bills, if your life is filled with broken relationships, if despair and depression haunt you, end-times theology promises a future free from pain and brokenness. It promises a place of healing where no one goes without, a new world where tears are wiped away. It promises that death and sorrow and mourning are no more—at least as long as you're a true believer.

So what if you have to believe in some quirky things and trust in eccentric people making wild predictions and proclamations? If that's all it takes to find peace and happiness, why wouldn't you go along with it? If simply believing in what they said meant that you, too, could be a part of a new heaven and new earth, why not?

The rapture may be a relatively new invention, but the promise of something better is as old as faith itself. Since the dawn of Christianity, people have believed that the return of Jesus was imminent and have sought to understand what that means and how they should prepare. For all its quirkiness, end-times theology is a natural extension of that quest to see faith become sight. End-times theology exists to prove why that faith is true. The predictions and proclamations are often over the top, if not simply delusional, but they spring from that same fount, from the desire for a better life. End-times theology not only promises that better life is coming; it also shows how and even when it's going to arrive.

It's intoxicating for a lot of people.

I know.

I was once one of them.

5

Losing My Religion

In eighth grade I found myself at yet another annual youth event. The event lasted through the weekend, with a concert on Saturday night put on by the wonderfully named band Brian White and Justice. It was an epic show, at least in the eyes of a sheltered thirteen-year-old boy who had never been to a real concert. So obviously it was objectively epic.

At the end of the show, there was an altar call. Because, well, of course there was. Guess who showed up for the altar call? That same preacher from children's camp. Just kidding. That would have been super weird.

It was God.

And this time I was pretty sure it actually *was* God. Because when I found myself kneeling down to pray with my youth pastor, I realized that it wasn't guilt that dragged me down the crimson red carpet of the sanctuary to kneel at an old wooden altar. A real sense of calling had invited me there. Maybe the bright lights and electric guitars and Brian White's testimony had helped. Or maybe it was actually the movement of the Holy Spirit—or maybe it was all of the above. Whoever or whatever it was, I felt a clear and definitive sense of calling that night to give my life to God. Not to just get saved again—I had already taken care of that a fiftieth or sixtieth time earlier that year at a Christian haunted house or "judgment house," where scary scenes like horrific drunk driving accidents are used (effectively in my case) to try to scare you into getting saved before you die and it's too late to save your soul from hell. I was at the altar that night, accepting a calling to ministry, because I *wanted* to be down there. I wanted to answer God's calling because I wanted to pour my life into the lives of others the way so many pastors and church people had poured their lives into mine.

I knelt at the altar pressure free that night. I felt no guilt, just a sense that I was finally on the right track—that maybe I was doing what I was meant to do. From that day forward, I knew I was going into ministry. But not just any ministry. I wanted to be a youth pastor. I was more sure about that than anything else I had ever been sure about. I would head to college knowing, beyond a shadow of a doubt, that God had called me to be a youth pastor.

Answering a call

Well, that and playing in the NBA. I came home from that youth event and immediately told my mom that God had called me. "To what?" she asked.

To being a youth pastor . . . and playing in the NBA. She smiled, as all moms do, no doubt torn between being proud of me for trying to answer God's call for my life and trying not to laugh at a slow, barely coordinated skinny white kid who couldn't jump but thought he was going to make it to the NBA.

Delusional or not, I spent the next several years preparing to do both, until a broken ankle and the reality of my limited talent put an end to my NBA dreams. With athletic stardom officially off the table, I prepared for my actual calling as much as I could. This amounted to telling everyone who asked about my future that I wanted to be a youth pastor—including my teachers at school, particularly in classes that I deemed irrelevant to my career goals.

On the first day of my junior year of high school, my pre-calculus teacher asked us to write down why we were taking the class. My answer? "Because it is required by the state in order to graduate. I am going into youth ministry, and this class has absolutely no bearing on my future plans." Thankfully, my teacher was a fellow Christian who fully supported my ministerial aspirations and was also equally full of grace—enough to overlook the insufferable arrogance of youth.

But I did take a few practical steps to prepare to be a youth pastor. I was active in my school's chapter of Fellowship of Christian Athletes, and when the time came, I ran for and was elected president—a role I pursued because in my mind it was basically like being a teenage youth pastor. I also made sure to never miss a mission trip. Sure, I loved the mission trip experience itself, but if I was going to be leading those some day, I needed to be prepared. How better to be prepared to lead a mission trip than by taking at least one every single summer from the time I was in seventh grade until my junior year of college? And whenever the opportunity came to testify on a mission trip, I took it. I'd transform my testimony to the group into a mini sermon, making sure to put the fear of being left behind and going to hell into the hearts of whoever was stuck having to listen to me.

As with many other high schools, mine had a job shadow day for seniors. Naturally, I chose to shadow my youth pastor, Tony. Guess how many other people shadowed pastors that day? Somewhere between zero and none—which should have made for an awkward moment when I had to stand up in front of the entire school after all the other job fields had been called and explain why my choice didn't fit into any of those categories. But I was so proud that awkwardness never even crossed my mind. I thought the rest of the students were suckers because I had the coolest job shadow day ever. (For the record, I was right. I had way more fun that day than I should have been allowed to get school credit for.)

When it finally came time to apply for college, I knew two things: one, I wanted to be a religion major; and two, I wanted to get as far away from home as possible. But my college needed to be a Christian school, and not just any Christian school. It needed to be a Nazarene school, because I couldn't trust what kind of liberal theology might be taught somewhere else.

The choice was easy. The Church of the Nazarene had a school on the opposite side of the country in San Diego, California. Point Loma Nazarene University sits right on top of a bluff overlooking the Pacific Ocean. You can stare at the Pacific while you eat lunch in the cafeteria and go surfing between classes. The baseball team can watch their home runs sail into the ocean. It seemed like the perfect place for a teenager itching to get as far away from home as possible.

But when it came time to turn in my application, I hesitated. Point Loma was beautiful. It was far away from home and, most importantly, down the street from an In-N-Out

Burger. But then a still, small voice started talking as I filled out my application. Maybe it was the Holy Spirit, but it may just have been my burning desire to know everything and be the smartest. In my mind, Trevecca Nazarene University, in my hometown of Nashville, had a better religion department, and all I cared about was taking the best religion classes possible so I could learn as much as possible and show everyone how smart I was.

Trevecca may indeed have had the better religion department. But it was just as likely that I *thought* it did because I was familiar with it. I had practically grown up on campus. Most of my family had gone to college there, half of them worked there, and the church I attended was on campus. Either way, it was a genuinely tough decision for me. I desperately wanted to get away from home, but at the same time I was terrified of not following God's will for my life, which I understood to be like the biblical prophecy of Jack Van Impe: a predetermined but veiled road map, decipherable only through clues I had to figure out in order to go to the right place, do the right things, get the right job, marry the right person, and make God happy.

I wrestled long and hard with the decision and spent countless hours in prayer. In the end, my application to Point Loma never left the small desk in my bedroom. I chose Trevecca. Partly because I really did think it offered me the best preparation for ministry, but also probably because all my friends were going there. Desperate as I was to get out of Nashville, I was too much of a coward to move across the country by myself.

That's how I ended up in Biblical Exegesis with Dr. Dan Spross at seven thirty in the morning. It was the very first class I ever took in college, and it was even less exciting than it sounds. I hated it. In my mind, college was going to be like

AP Sunday school. I'd had all the answers in regular Sunday school, so AP Sunday school was obviously going to be a breeze.

Unprepared

How wrong I was.

And not just because college turned out to be nothing like Sunday school. Taking Biblical Exegesis as my first class in college was a mistake. I was woefully unprepared for the rigors of college life. Hell-bent on signing up for religion classes as soon as possible, I had taken as many AP exams and CLEP tests as I could during high school so that I could skip most or even all of my general education classes. My plan succeeded. I entered college academically as a sophomore, which meant I could immediately start taking religion classes normally reserved for real sophomores after they got their feet wet doing real college work. I didn't care about any of that, but I should have. Jumping that quickly into the deep end of the pool meant I never got to wade through the shallow end of Gen Ed classes. I never got to learn how to learn in college, how to write in college, or how to accept the fact that college isn't like high school.

So when I crossed the linoleum threshold that first morning of college and sat down for my first Biblical Exegesis class, my expectations of religion classes were shattered. Instead of getting candy for answering questions about the Bible, we were handed a three-hundred-page book and told to write a ten-page paper about it by the following Monday. I was crestfallen. When class was over, I went into a tailspin about whether this ministry thing was something I actually wanted to do. Not because the professor did anything wrong. Far from it. In fact, by the time I graduated, he ended up becoming one of my favorite professors in college. I simply wasn't expecting my religion classes to be that hard, that rigorous, and to be honest, that boring.

What you've got to understand is that, as ridiculous as it sounds, I really had been looking forward to this class and New Testament Theology and Introduction to New Testament Greek and all the other religion classes. In my mind, I really did think they were going to be like Sunday school, except more fun, because we would be getting into all the deep theological stuff we usually skipped over in Sunday school because there wasn't enough time or interest from my classmates in discussing the minute details of penal substitution atonement. But most importantly, I thought religion classes were finally going to give me all the academic ammunition I needed to figure out the end times and shoot down anyone who disagreed with me. But my religion classes weren't anything like that. There was redaction criticism to learn about, and Greek verbs to conjugate, and educational theories to learn, and I hated it.

All of it.

That first semester was a war of attrition, and I was very quickly becoming the vanquished foe. But there was hope in the form of a meeting I had with the New Testament professor, who also happened to be my advisor. We had to meet to arrange my schedule for the spring semester. For most normal students, this would have been a boring meeting just as soon to be avoided. For me, it was the opportunity of a lifetime. It was my chance to have all my ideas about the end times confirmed, all my questions about the rapture answered—by a real bona fide expert.

A map that doesn't exist

As I sat outside my advisor's office that afternoon, my heart was racing in anticipation as if I were a kid on my way to Disney World for the first time. In my mind I was. In my mind, religion professors had the greatest job imaginable. They got paid to sit around and talk about theology all day! How could life get any better than that? Their offices had to be the happiest places on earth.

But that wasn't the only reason I was excited to be there that day. I couldn't wait to show off my theological brilliance, impress my professor, and win his undying admiration for how astutely I understood the mysteries of the end times. I don't think I had even sat down on the old cloth-covered chair in his office before I began assailing him with my dispensational theories and questions. I didn't take another breath for at least twenty minutes. Every theory I had I shared. Every suspect for the Antichrist I named. Every Israel-related news event I dissected. When I was finally done, I looked at my advisor and said, "So what do you think?" He cracked a sly grin, as if this wasn't the first time he had heard this sort of thing and I hadn't just blown his mind with my incredible insights into the end times.

And then he spoke.

I was expecting affirmation of my expertise, maybe a little bit of clarity on my prophetic timetables, or at least a phone call to the department chair letting him know my advisor was so impressed by my genius that I would be joining the faculty. What I got instead was something else entirely. In a calm, patient voice he said, "You know, Jack Van Impe seems like a smart guy to me. But the problem I have with him, and folks like him, is they're trying to pinpoint places on a map that simply doesn't exist. They're right: we are living in the end times. But we have been ever since Jesus walked out of the tomb." I'd never been so stunned into silence. I felt like the emperor with no clothes, dragged out before the masses. My apocalyptic delusions had been laid bare. Sensing my embarrassment, my advisor quietly signed my class schedule and gently sent me on my way.

What happened next was a whirlwind of shock, confusion, and anger. I locked myself in my dorm room until I could find the courage to show my face in public again. I immediately went into denial mode. My professor may have had my undying respect as an authority on all things biblical before that meeting, but I had barely made it out of his office before deciding he was a fool. He had to be. The end times were so clear! The fulfillment of prophecies in the news was so obvious. Maybe if I could just get him to watch one episode of *Jack Van Impe Presents* he would understand. Maybe he'd get it and come over to my side, to the side of truth, the side of Jesus.

The denial lasted for days, weeks, months even. When I finally began to make space in my head for the possibility that maybe, just maybe, a guy with a PhD in New Testament knew what he was talking about, the denial slowly began to fade. It was replaced by anger. I was mad. Really, really mad. At first, my anger was directed squarely at my professor. Why couldn't he have just gone along with what I said? Why couldn't he have just politely smiled, nodded, and sent me on my way? My ignorance had been bliss. Who did he think he was, anyway? Oh right, an expert in the New Testament.

Just accepting that simple fact took far longer than it should have. After all, the very reason I was so excited to share my end-times ideas with him was my respect for his biblical expertise. But acknowledging that he knew more than I did wasn't just about my arrogance, though that certainly played a role. Acknowledging he knew more than I did meant admitting he was right and I was wrong—not just about some random topic, but about a core tenet of my faith, a defining part of my identity.

If I had been so wrong about the mysteries of the end times, then maybe I wasn't quite as smart as I thought I was. Simply accepting that possibility—that I could be wrong about something I was so sure I was right about—took countless weeks and months of self-reflection. Forcing myself to confront the reality that maybe I didn't have everything figured out was hard. I was still angry with my advisor, but I still trusted my other religion professors, so I turned to them for leads on books I could read and biblical experts I could consult to prove how wrong my advisor had been. They obliged, but I didn't find the proof I wanted to shove in his face. Worse still, those biblical experts all agreed with him.

When I finally came around to accepting the fact that I was wrong, the anger didn't subside. It simply began to be directed elsewhere: toward Jack and Rexella, toward Jerry Jenkins and Tim LaHaye, toward anyone and everyone who had ever suckered me into believing in end-times prophecy and the rapture. How could they have tricked me into something like that and made me look like a complete fool in front of my professor?

Eventually my anger turned inward. After all, if anyone was to blame for all of this, it was me. I was the sucker. How could I have been so naïve? So gullible? So dumb? My whole life I had prided myself on having all the Sunday school answers, being the top Bible quizzer at church, and knowing everything there was to know about the Christian faith. At that moment, I couldn't have felt any dumber, and it was that embarrassment that turned to rage.

But being the nerdy church kid I was, that rage didn't turn into anything scandalous. It turned into petty, childish protests only recognizable to me. Why? Because while I may have begun to have my doubts about the rapture, I was still terrified of hell, and I didn't want to do anything that would have completely jeopardized my soul.

My rebellion was cliché. Super, incredibly, ridiculously cliché. I stopped doing my homework. (Like I said, super, incredibly, ridiculously cliché.) I got a D in my second semester of New Testament Greek after turning in all of one assignment that semester, so I felt like a rebel. I had stuck it to the Man! For a while, at least. But then I lost my academic scholarships and found myself torn between the love of feeling like a rebel and the terror of massive student loans.

The next step in my grand plan of rebellion was to stop going to chapel. Again, super cliché, but it felt hardcore to a kid who never missed church. Ever. Chapel was held three times a week. I started going zero times a week—or if I did go, I sat in the back and took a nap. Such a rebel. Unfortunately for me, the school's threat of penalties for missing too many chapel services wasn't a bluff. I racked up several hundred dollars in fines, and had it not been for the grace of the assistant dean—who, after I groveled in his office on bended knee, reduced my penalty to a more manageable dollar figure—I would have had to take out another student loan to pay for them.

But there was still church to skip.

To be fair, lots of churchgoing kids skip church when they go off to college, if for no other reason than that Mom and Dad aren't around to make them go. But I relished it, staying as far away from church and anything resembling church as I could.

Then I changed my major.

I held on to the religion part, because I still liked studying religion. But I wanted nothing to do with the practical, ministry-oriented classes. Because I had started college academically as a sophomore, I had time to burn. (At least I thought I did; I failed to realize that graduating in three years instead of four would have saved me a huge chunk of money.) So I took on a double major: history and political science. My thought was twofold: this double major was the closest thing our school had to a prelaw program, and being a lawyer seemed like the furthest thing from being a pastor. Plus, I had seen *A Few Good Men* a whole bunch of times and figured it would be a cakewalk.

I know this will come as a shock, but it wasn't.

So I tried getting a tattoo—a religious one, of course. I chose the symbol known as the Chi-Rho, formed from the first two letters, *X* and *P*, for "Christ" in Greek. I made sure to get it tattooed on the hardest of hardcore places: my ankle, because "how beautiful upon the mountains are the feet" and all that (Isaiah 52:7). Then I got a few piercings. When that didn't solve my spiritual crisis either, I took a trip across the country to Yellowstone to find myself. All I found there were sore feet and exhaustion from a hiking excursion for which I was woefully unprepared.

By the time all was said and done, I was still as bitter and angry as ever. If anything, my newfound doubt about the rapture was just the first loose thread to be pulled. The rest of my faith began to unravel as well. After all, if I had been wrong about the rapture, what else had I been wrong about? A lot, it turned out. It would take me several years to find out just how much I was wrong about and how many people I had unfairly passed judgment on.

I might have seen it all coming had I paid just a bit more attention in my advisor's Introduction to Biblical Faith class. On one of the very first days of class, he gave us a warning about where our religious studies would lead. Had I paid attention, I might have been able to see my crisis of faith coming over the horizon. I heard the words he said—that's why I can tell you about it now—but back then I was too arrogant to think it ever could or would apply to me.

Before we dived into actually studying the Bible or the nuts and bolts of the Christian faith, our professor warned us that what we would be studying would likely challenge some of the things we thought we knew about the Bible and Christianity. We might be uncomfortable with, or even mad at, some of the things suggested in class or claimed by the authors we would read. We would encounter ideas that ran counter to what we always thought we knew to be true.

But that was okay, he said. Even though what we were learning would probably be painful, it was all a normal part of the learning process. This learning process, according to French philosopher Paul Ricœur, can be best understood in three stages.[1]

First naiveté

The first stage of the process is called the first naiveté. This is the precritical stage of our understanding or knowledge of the world, in which we accept what we are taught without giving it much critical thought or attention. For me, that would have been the Sunday school period of my life—or really all my time growing up and learning something in church. I implicitly trusted the people charged with teaching me the faith. Not that I shouldn't have; none of them had any nefarious intent to mislead me. But I trusted my Sunday school teachers and the adults in my life without question. Whenever they told me something about the Bible or Jesus or God, I believed that whatever they said was true.

Most of us do the same when we're young. And more of us than we care to admit stay in this stage long after we grow up. A not-insignificant number of us never really grow out of it. Need proof? Just take a look at your social media feed and see how many people regularly share information that is clearly incorrect but that they take to be the gospel truth because the source seems authoritative. Some of that is the result of confirmation bias—something even the most educated and wise can fall victim to. But when we accept the word of an authority figure simply because of their perceived authority and without question or reflection, we're likely still living in the first naiveté.

Critical reflection

One of the core purposes of higher education is to move students out of the first naiveté and into the next stage of learning and understanding: critical reflection. You might also call it the humbling stage. That is just me talking, not Ricœur. But for me, the biggest lesson from the critical reflection stage isn't the knowledge you gain—though that is certainly important. It's the humility that comes as your eyes are opened up to how much you don't know and how arrogant you were in your naiveté.

Now to be clear, this usually isn't an overnight realization. When you first get to the critical reflection stage, it's rough and embarrassing. My rapture-shattering conversation with my advisor was my baptism by fire into critical reflection. I didn't leave his office joyful over my newfound enlightenment; I left angry and embarrassed. And I stayed that way for a long, long time.

Had I paid attention that first day in Introduction to Biblical Faith, perhaps this stage wouldn't have lasted quite so long. After all, my professor had tried to warn me. He had tried to prepare me for the inevitable moment when I would come face-to-face with indisputable proof that a belief that I was once so sure was right was actually wrong. When that time came, I wouldn't be able to do the mental gymnastics necessary to wiggle out of it. When that time came, he warned, I had a choice to make. I could bury my head in the sand, refuse to believe it, and live the rest of my life in willfully ignorant denial (kind of like if Neo had chosen to take the blue pill and plug back into the Matrix). Or I could continue down the road of discovery and learning, no matter how hard or scary or painful it might be.

The path of willful ignorance is easy, comfortable, and known. It's filled with plenty of fellow travelers, because many take it. But more than a few choose the more difficult path—or, like me, many find themselves forced onto it, because intellectual integrity eventually leaves them with no other choice.

I say *eventually*, because when the door to critical reflection was first opened, I didn't run through. I slammed it shut and ran as hard as I could the other way. I tried going back to living in the first naiveté—tried as hard as I could to ignore the bad theology and contradictions of dispensationalism whenever they reared their ugly head. I tried to take the blue pill, but it was too late. It took many bitter months—years, actually—to accept the truth when I saw it and to forgive both those who taught me the wrong things and myself for believing them. Again, those folks had not intentionally led me astray, so they didn't need my forgiveness for that. I needed to forgive them in the sense of letting go of the idea that they had tried to trick me, in the sense of letting go of the belief that there was some secret cabal that had colluded to embarrass me in college. Even though I knew, intellectually, that they were good, well-meaning people who were simply trying to teach me what they believed to be true, accepting that simple truth in my soul took a long time.

It took even longer for me to forgive myself. I'd always prided myself on being the smartest guy in the room. I still do—even though I'm now keenly aware of how rarely, if ever, that is true. But pride is a difficult thing to overcome. They say pride cometh before the fall, and it did. But it also came along with me for the ride. Even as the pieces of my faith eventually began to be put back together, the pain and embarrassment of realizing just how arrogant I had been in my youth lingered. It still does. It was years before I could even talk about my previous devotion to the end times without embarrassment-induced rage building up inside me.

Second naiveté

Thankfully, the anger eventually subsided. It has to if you're going to move on to the third and final stage of understanding. You need a healthy dose of humility to move on to what Ricœur calls the second naiveté. You need it because the second naiveté requires you to accept what you don't know along with the mysteries you can't figure out. It's not a return to willful ignorance but rather an embrace of the fact that you don't have everything figured out and that's okay. That doesn't mean you stop trying to pursue knowledge and understanding. Rather, you learn to drop the need to know everything, to learn every fact and decipher every mystery.

This is where a healthy faith lives: in a place of critical reflection that pursues the greatest depths of knowledge, accepts the things found there, and keeps diving deeper, but without the delusion of ever thinking we have it all figured out. The delusion is replaced with humility—a humility that recognizes our own limits and ignorance and sees the limits and ignorance of others not as a chance to embarrass them but as an opportunity to show them the same sort of grace and understanding that others have extended to us.

If you've found yourself in this stage of life, hopefully that humility is something you're willing to share. I hope you're not shy about talking about what you've gone through, no matter how humbling the learning process might have been. The church is in desperate need of your story of humility and growth because it's also in desperate need of people who, unlike me, don't hate admitting that they're wrong about things. Most people are like that, but I've made thinking I'm right into something of an art form. Don't get me wrong: my "rightness" complex is not something I'm particularly proud of. I'd like to think I've become more comfortable with admitting when I'm wrong, but you'd have to ask my wife to know how true that actually is.

Admitting I was wrong

The conservative evangelicalism I grew up in was, and still is, a world of certainty. If something was wrong, it was wrong all the time. Murky areas were for squishy heathen liberals— moral relativists who couldn't make up their minds about anything because they were too committed to being nice to speak the truth.

"The Bible says it. I believe it. That settles it!" was my mantra. I had verses for everything, proof texts to prove why I was right and why you were living in sin. The idea that I could have been misunderstanding any of those verses, or taking any of them out of context, never entered my mind. I considered myself a biblical interpretations savant at the age of fourteen. Right and wrong beliefs were so obvious! If Christianity was about having all the right answers, it wasn't because you needed to search for them. It was because you just needed to accept them. Believe in the right things and you, too, would have all the right answers and would go to heaven. The answers were right there in the Bible or a sermon or a Sunday school lesson. It was my job as a Christian to tell the rest of the world why they were wrong and why being wrong had them on a one-way trip to hell.

When you grow up thinking the Christian life is about knowing all the right answers, dispensationalism seems all the more appealing. It offered answers to things I wasn't supposed to be able to have answers to: the end of the world and the timing of Jesus' return.

I don't have to tell you all the problems that come with a worldview that thinks it has all the answers. Arrogance, of course, is chief among them. Faith becomes a point of pride, because in this paradigm faith isn't trust in God; it's having all the right answers. Faith becomes superiority over the ignorant and the lost, and humility is transformed from a Christlike virtue to a deadly sin. To acknowledge the possibility of being wrong is to open up a breach in the well-constructed defenses of doctrinal surety.

Not only did the words "I might be wrong" never enter my mind; to have said those words would have felt like a sin. Which makes a sort of perverse sense. If right answers and right belief are the path to salvation, being wrong is a sin that paves the path to hell. Not just literally. At times, actual hell would have been preferable to the hell of personal embarrassment whenever I was exposed as being wrong in front of others. That's exactly what I went through when I came face-to-face with the truth about the rapture: it felt like my own personal hell of embarrassment and self-doubt. This wasn't my professor's fault. It was mine for being so arrogant as to think not only that I had all the right answers but that I couldn't possibly be wrong.

That's why it took me so long to emerge from that hell. Any sort of life-altering self-realization takes a while to work through, of course. But I was coming out of a world-view that treated even the consideration of other points of view—at least about large theological issues—and the potential doubt that consideration might cause, to be noth-ing short of sinful. So if I was told by a person in authority that Muslims, LGBT people, alcohol, or rock music were sinful and here's a Bible verse to prove it, I never thought to question it. If ever there was a moment when I did, I felt guilty for doubting the truth.

It's this certainty—that we already have everything figured out and never need to consider the possibility that we might have been wrong about something or somebody—that stands as one of the greatest challenges the church faces today, par-ticularly in light of globalization. As the world shrinks, we're forced to come face-to-face with people who are different from us and on whose anonymity we could previously project all our prejudices. As science comes alongside globalization, its insights and revelations about how the world works can pour water on the fire of our conviction of who is dangerous and what is unnatural. So we have a choice to make. We can either break bread with our new neighbors and listen to what they have to say or we can continue to find reasons to hate them for being different from us. We can open ourselves up to the idea that not only could we have been wrong, but maybe the Holy Spirit is at work in our lives the way the Spirit was with Peter and his vision of the sheet filled with unclean food that he was commanded to eat (Acts 10:9-16). Or we can further entrench ourselves in our preconceived notions about the world and the people in it. We could consider that perhaps the Spirit is opening our eyes, as she did with Peter, to deeper truths about the world. Or we can reject that possibility, double down on our beliefs, and seek out proof texts to prove we were right all along.

Far too many of us have chosen to do the latter—to willfully live in the first naiveté. Admitting that we're wrong either is too painful or is seen as sinful. And so arrogance becomes the sinew of our faith. It's this elemental arrogance that has the church mired in a reputation of bigotry, hatefulness, and ignorance. For too long we've refused to make space for even the possibility that we might be wrong about anything. In the name of God, we've refused to make space for the people Jesus went out of his way to invite to the table of God. It's this sort of sanctified arrogance that leads to an us-versus-them mentality that sees the world as a battlefield instead of a home. Our neighbors become our enemies. We dehumanize them simply because they don't think or talk or believe or act exactly the way we do.

Learning to say "I don't know"

As Paul reminds us in the timeless hymn of Philippians 2, we are called to imitate Christ's humility, to have in us the sort of Christlike humility that values others above ourselves, so that we are looking not to our own interests but rather to the interests of others. We're called to love people more than we love being right, but being right theologically rather than being in right relationship with our neighbor has become the defining identity of the church.

Sometimes that call to Christlike humility means acknowledging we're wrong, but other times it's as simple as saying "I don't know." Unfortunately, we don't make much room in the church for "I don't know" either, especially when it comes to our leaders. We expect them to have all the answers, all the time, and to give them to us whenever we ask, like they are some sort of theological Google-made-flesh. When right belief is the key to salvation, there is simply no space for *not* knowing.

Even after years of wandering in the spiritual wilderness, graduating from college, doing a graduate degree in theology that humbled me even more, and spending years of ministry with teenagers that humbled me still more—even after all that, I was still terrified of three little words: *I don't know.*

As a minister, I had to be prepared to proclaim the gospel "in season and out," as Paul commanded in 2 Timothy 4:2 (NIV). I thought I couldn't do that without having all the answers, because that's what the gospel was about to me: the right answers. So I had to have an answer ready at all times—or else make up something that sounded good. The idea of admitting I didn't know was horrifying, a mini hell of embarrassment and shame. As a youth pastor, the fear was even more crippling. I was tasked with teaching teenagers the faith. In my mind, that meant I had to give them the answers and direction they needed to be good disciples. How could I do that if I didn't have the answer to every question they asked?

When I finally found the courage to admit that even as a pastor, I didn't know everything, and that I even had doubts about some of the things I said I believed, it felt like a giant burden was lifted off my shoulders. My admission also opened the floodgates, as friends and strangers alike began sharing their own questions, insecurities, and doubts.

It turned out I wasn't alone. And not only was I not alone, I was probably in the majority. Most people in the church struggle with doubt and uncertainty at some point in their lives. Little did I know how many people sitting in the pews next to me at church were wrestling with the same doubts and questions that I was—including many standing behind the pulpit. We just didn't want to admit it, let alone talk about it.

Sadly, we don't make a lot of space for folks with questions. We silently shame them if they don't have the right answers, ask too many questions, or refuse to join the right side on cultural or theological debates. Many mainline denominations and progressive traditions have made embracing doubters a kind of calling card. But in the sort of conservative, fundamentalist Christianity I grew up in, having all the right answers and never wavering in your faith were the marks of a true Christian. (Well, that and never having a beer.)

Holy doubt

We have forgotten the long and sacred history of doubt and struggle with faith in the church, going back long before there was something called the church.

The Old Testament is filled with stories of people who struggled with their faith. Abraham doubted God's faithfulness to give him a promised heir. Moses doubted God would provide for the people in the wilderness. Elijah doubted God's faithfulness. So did Job. When we get to the New Testament, we find twelve doubting disciples—including their leader, Peter, who doubted Jesus when he called him out to walk on the water. On the cross, Jesus took on the cry of the psalmist and doubters everywhere when he cried out to God, "My God, my God, why have you forsaken me?" (Matthew 27:46; cf. Mark 15:34; Psalm 22:1). After the crucifixion, the disciples hid in fear with no hope that things were going to get better. Even after the resurrection, Thomas doubted it was true until Jesus invited him to put his fingers in the holes of his hands.

But the spiritual struggles of the faithful didn't stop with the Bible. After it became apparent that Jesus wasn't coming back as soon as people expected, many in the early church had doubts about whether he was going to come back at all—so much so that the book of Revelation became something of an embarrassment to many Christians. In the Middle Ages, Saint John of the Cross endured what he called the "dark night of the soul." In the modern era, that great pillar of faith Mother Teresa confessed, in her posthumously released diary, that she experienced tremendous doubts, including going some fifty years without feeling the presence of God in her life. Read that last line again. Mother Teresa—the person whose name has become synonymous with faithful Christianity—struggled with crippling doubt for fifty years. Half a century. Most of her adult life.

But in many corners of Christianity today, particularly within fundamentalism where dispensationalism thrives, doubt is treated as a sin. To doubt is to call into question both God and the authority of the church. The former is treated as blasphemy and the latter as an intolerable threat to the established order (or, more specifically, the people leading that established order). The Christian faith may have a long history of doubters, and the writers of the Bible may have gone out of their way to note doubt's often-unavoidable place in our spiritual journey. But in many corners of the church today, doubt is treated as a betrayal of God's love. If we really loved God, the logic goes, then we would never doubt God's presence, God's faithfulness, or the people who tell us they've been called by God to lead us.

When doubt becomes a scarlet letter in the church, one of three things results: 1) people are lost to their arrogance; 2) people live in agony, tormented in the shadows; or 3) people simply leave the church. The first and second—people living in arrogance, on the one hand, and others living in shame because of their doubts—have been going on forever. But we're starting to see the third—people leaving the church—pick up steam each year. In the past decade alone, the Southern Baptist Convention, the largest Protestant denomination in the United States, lost a million members.[2] Of course, not everyone is leaving because of doubts and questions. Some people have the space to ask questions in church and still leave, for myriad reasons. But in the information age, when people quite literally carry around the totality of human knowledge in their pocket, we in the church can't afford to pretend we know everything. We can no longer claim we have everything figured out all the time.

We need to remember the example of Jesus. He didn't chase Thomas away or chastise him for his doubt. He embraced him.

When Peter faltered on the sea, Jesus didn't let him drown. He reached out, picked him up, and carried him back to the boat, where he wasn't greeted by shame but by fellow disciples whose own doubts were far stronger than his own—so strong, in fact, that they didn't even have enough faith to get out of the boat. And when Jesus ascended into heaven, leaving his disciples behind with the great commission to go and make disciples of all the nations on earth, some still doubted. But Jesus didn't excommunicate them. He gave them the same authority as the rest of the disciples to be his agents of grace in the world (Matthew 28:16-20).

The story of God's people is the story of people who struggle with their faith, yet aren't pushed away or chastised by God. Instead, we are given the grace to keep going, to keep doing the work of bringing the kingdom of God to earth as it is in heaven. Unfortunately, instead of embracing doubts, we often draw ideological lines in the sand and demand allegiance to our theological convictions. That approach might rally our base in the beginning. But silencing doubt and shaming people for asking too many questions—labeling them as "creating disunity"—ultimately ends up driving people away, often permanently.

The church's intolerance of doubt almost drove me away. When I lost my faith in the rapture, I thought that I had lost my faith altogether. For a long time I thought that there was no room for me in the Christian faith if I didn't have everything figured out or know all the right answers. That sense of spiritual homelessness spurred so much of my anger and embarrassment. I wasn't just embarrassed because I had made a fool of myself in front of a professor I respected. I was angry because I thought that, in having all those answers taken away,

I'd had my faith taken away from me as well. If Christianity was all about belief and if I didn't have the right beliefs, who was I? What else was there left worth believing in?

The church has inflicted far too much pain on people by not making space for their questions and doubt. However, making space for people who doubt and wrestle with their faith isn't about keeping people on the membership rolls and maintaining church attendance figures. Making space for people who doubt and wrestle with their faith is critical to the life of the church because faith is found in doubt. Without doubt, faith wouldn't be faith. It would simply be knowledge. Knowledge may sound more appealing and powerful—it sure did to me when I was in love with the rapture. But Jesus said blessed are those who have not seen and yet still believe, not blessed are those who already have it all figured out (see John 20:29).

We seem to have forgotten that we see in a mirror dimly. One day we will see clearly, but that day is not today. And that's okay, because we're called to faith, not expertise. If we had all the answers it wouldn't be faith; it would be something more akin to science. As wonderful as science is, we have to resist the urge to turn the Christian faith into a scientific system. We need to let science be science and faith be faith. Learning and understanding are in no way bad; in fact, they are a gift of the Holy Spirit. But when we try to force the round peg of faith into the square hole of science, not only do we strip faith of its mystery but, more importantly, we strip it of its boundless beauty.

The beauty of Christianity isn't in its theological systems and dogmatic rules. It's in the ability of faith as small as a tiny mustard seed to move mountains, love the unlovable, and bring heaven to earth. When we try to bind the Christian faith to the affirmation of ideology and dogma, we strip it of its life-giving, creation-transforming power. Faith is about transformation, not affirmation. It's about believing that no matter how flawed we are, how riddled with doubt we might be, how broken and sinful our lives may have become, God loves us anyway. Faith is believing that God is working through us to do a new and wonderful thing in the world, not just for our sake but for all of creation.

Doubt isn't something in need of fixing. It's not a disease the church needs to cure. It's a part of faith. It's a step in all our journeys, much like Ricœur's critical thinking stage. Doubt may even be a constant lifelong companion for some of us, just as it has been for so many saints throughout the history of the Christian faith. As the church, we must resist the urge to fight doubt with answers. We certainly must stop shaming people, whether overtly or covertly, for asking questions and having doubts about what they believe. Certainty is not the key to salvation. As Anne Lamott famously says, "The opposite of faith is not doubt, but certainty. Certainty is missing the point entirely. Faith includes noticing the mess, the emptiness and discomfort, and letting it be there until some light returns. Faith also means reaching deeply within, for the sense one was born with, the sense, for example, to go for a walk."[3]

To those words of wisdom I would only add this: that walk is one we do together, because faith is something we do together. Faith is a way of living together, not a moment of individual intellectual assent. That's why there's room for doubt. If any of us struggle to stand up in the chaotic waters of faith and life, the rest of us carry them until they can stand on their own again. The way we do that—the way we carry each other and find the strength to keep going—isn't with answers, certainty, or dogma. It's through hope. Hope that things are going to get better. Hope that God is at work in the world. Hope that we live out each and every day until our faith becomes sight.

That's what makes the Christian faith good news.

And that's the story of Revelation.

6

Couch-Skiing

You probably don't remember the story of how any of your friends met their spouses, but I bet you'll never forget how I met mine.

It was a cold, wintery night, thanks to a rare-for-Nashville blanket of snow. I was smack dab in the middle of my college campus, getting ready to be dragged behind my friend's Jeep on a couch—naked.

See? I told you my memory would be seared into your imagination. Sorry about that.

Anyway, earlier that day my friend Mike had gotten together with a couple of other guys from our dorm, and through what can only be described as a stroke of divine inspiration, got the brilliant idea to take an old couch out of their dorm room, nail a set of skis to the bottom of it, and tie the newly created "ski couch" to the back of his Jeep Grand Cherokee with a ski rope.

They had spent the afternoon taking turns couch-skiing across campus when my opportunity to join in the wintery hijinks finally arrived. I, too, had what can only be described as a stroke of divine inspiration and got the brilliant idea to ride on the couch naked. Okay, maybe that wasn't divine inspiration so much as the stupidity of youth combined with a need for attention. But there I was—ski goggles on, shirt off, and almost fully disrobed—when my friend Nathan showed up to join us. He wasn't alone. He had brought a friend with him. Her name was Kim, and they were both eager to go couch-skiing too. Of course, they were less eager to go when they learned of my plan to ski in the buff. So being the gentleman that I was, I agreed to keep my boxers on for the ride.

It was love at first sight.

Okay, maybe it wasn't quite love at first sight. Although, to be fair, it never could have been, because I couldn't see her through my fogged-up ski goggles. The only thing I could see was the vague form of my friend Nathan sitting in the middle of the couch between Kim and me—clearly to keep her as far away as possible from the moron whose company she had to endure if she wanted to go couch-skiing. My dignity tossed to the side, Mike started up the Jeep and off we went.

Across campus.

On a couch.

On skis.

Being dragged behind a Jeep.

It was more fun than one person should be allowed in this life—so much so that I didn't even notice the cold, at least not until Mike took a sharp turn. The couch swung too wide behind him, flipped over, and tossed the three of us into a snow bank.

Thankfully for me, couch-skiing wasn't the last time Kim and I saw each other. It was a while before we hung out again, but from time to time we would run into each other on campus and say hello. Then one day about a year later, while I was typing a paper on Mike's computer, an instant message popped up on his computer screen.

You remember AOL Instant Messenger, right? If not, then thanks for making me feel old. Instant Messenger was like texting before texting was a thing. You could only do it on your computer; phones weren't that fancy yet. But when I was in college, it was a great way to do some high-tech flirting. And flirt I did. Kim was looking for Mike that day, not me. But I was looking for a date. So as any young Christian man at a Christian college would do, I took the coincidence for what it obviously was: a sign from God.

So I asked her out.

Via Instant Messenger.

Which sounds really cheesy, but it was actually way cheesier than that. Being a young Christian man at a Christian college, I couldn't ask her out for drinks. So I asked her out for milkshakes. And before you make fun of me for asking her out for milkshakes, allow me to remind you how wonderful milkshakes are. Fine. So it was cheesy. But for some inexplicable reason she said yes. Later that week I picked her up to take her out for milkshakes at a local watering hole called Jackson's, which was filled with the kind of people who are way too cool to ask other people out for milkshakes. But I thought maybe Jackson's could balance out my complete inability to be suave and sophisticated.

I'm not sure it did, but Kim and I did hit it off. She was easy to talk to, and more importantly, she was really smart. I

loved talking to someone who could challenge me intellectually. Most of our first dates were spent just talking and getting
to know each other. On one date in particular we talked so
long we lost track of time, missed curfew, and she got locked
out of her dorm. So we ended up sitting on a swing in the
middle of campus, talking, until the sun came up and the res-
ident director unlocked the door. It was and still is one of our
favorite dates.

But Kim was much more than a good date. She was more,
even, than my future wife and the mother of our children. She
was my Aladdin, showing me a whole new way of looking at
the world.

They love Jesus too?

I met Kim after my faith had begun to be unraptured. For all
intents and purposes, though, I was still a dyed-in-the-wool
conservative Christian fundamentalist who thought that the
only true Christians were conservative Christians who always
voted Republican. Also, real Christians were mostly from the
South, where everyone still went to church on Sunday. There
were probably a few Christians in exile elsewhere, but not
many. They were all definitely conservative, Protestant, and
probably Nazarene too.

Kim was a Yankee, born and bred in New England. Worse,
she was a liberal. Worse still, she didn't like Chick-fil-A.
(Although she has come around on that last point.) To make
matters even more bewildering, her mom's side of the family
was liberal, and her dad, who had a longer Nazarene lineage
than I had, had converted to Catholicism after her parents'
divorce and started attending mass at a local monastery—and
was now training to become a Benedictine monk.

Worse *still*, they all loved Jesus.

I couldn't make heads or tails out of any of it.

On my list of people who definitely weren't Christian were Yankees (both the people and the team), liberals, and Catholics. In that order. Yet here were these people who not only said they loved Jesus and went to church as much as or more than I did—one of them had even taken Jesus seriously when he said sell everything you have and give it to the poor, then come follow me (see Matthew 19:21). Here I was, thinking I was the perfect Christian only to find out my girlfriend's dad was literally a monk. (He did drink beer and listen to secular music, though, so I called us even.)

In all seriousness, getting to know Kim had as profound an effect on my faith as did that embarrassing conversation in my professor's office years before. She and her family forced me to confront the reality of the conservative Christian bubble that I had grown up in and was largely still living inside. They forced me to face the truth that there are people out there who look different from me, talk differently from me, think differently from me, believe differently from me, don't like sweet tea and Chick-fil-A like me, and yet still love Jesus as much as or maybe even more than I do.

When I finally realized that what I thought was a heavenly choir shouting amen to all my beliefs was actually just a sanctified echo chamber, I began to see that a lot of the people I once considered my enemies were actually just my neighbors. Many of them were quite nice, decent people. It turned out that atheists weren't agents of the devil, that Muslims weren't all secret terrorists trying to force me to live under sharia law, that LGBT folks weren't godless degenerates trying to turn me gay, that poor people weren't a bunch of lazy moochers, and that people having a glass of wine with dinner weren't all raging alcoholics.

The further I stepped beyond my ideological bubble, the more my mind was blown. But more than anything else, as I left the echo chamber behind, I was finally forced to confront the truth about the rapture and why end-times theology wasn't just bad theology but a type of Christianity that had serious, real-world problems; problems I had helped spread not just through my words but also through my actions.

Missing from the Bible

The most fundamental problem with the rapture is that it never actually appears in the Bible.

This is true in two ways. In the most literal sense, the word *rapture* doesn't appear in any English translation of the Bible—and there are dozens of English translations. But it never did. There's no verse saying, "And then Jesus will rapture some folks," no offhand shout-out, not even a mention of the disciples feeling "enraptured."

"But the Bible wasn't written in English!" you say. That's a fair point, and one we don't take into consideration often enough when reading the Bible. We're more open to pulling out our own toenails than to thinking about the fact that some things from ancient languages are bound to be lost in translation, especially if you only speak one of the two languages being translated. (And if the language you do speak is largely confined to emojis and GIFs, things get even trickier.)

But here's the thing: even the concept of the rapture doesn't appear in the original Greek or Hebrew or in the smatterings of Aramaic found in the Bible. As we'll see shortly, the original Greek used in the New Testament passages cited as proof texts for the rapture make it clear that a rapture-like event is not what is being described by the biblical writers.

So if it's not in our English translations, or even in the original biblical languages, then where did the word *rapture* come from? Like so many things in Christian history, we can blame the Roman Empire for this one. At least indirectly. Long before the Bible was translated into English, it was translated into Latin, the language of the Roman Empire, and eventually the official language of the church. In Revelation 4:1, John is told to "come up here." In the Latin translation of that passage, the word *rapio* is used. Translated literally, *rapio* means "to snatch, grab, or take away."

Before the dawn of dispensationalism in the nineteenth century, no one gave much thought to that word. The idea of being taken away into the heavens was widely used in the context of an apocalyptic vision and was well established in the apocalyptic tradition. The person having the vision was often snatched up or taken away to the heavens to see whatever it was God (or the gods) wanted them to see. But then John Darby came along, bringing his dispensationalism along with him. Darby loved him some secret biblical codes and timetables. Soon, what was once a standard part of an apocalyptic vision (*rapio*, or being taken away to heaven) suddenly became a secret code for an event the Bible never mentions: the rapture.

That's not to say that the Bible doesn't mention anyone being taken up to heaven at the end of all things. It does, a couple of times. But dispensationalists have cut and pasted those passages together with Revelation 4:1 to create the rapture. The problem is, those passages aren't describing the rapture. As we already learned from 1 Corinthians 15:52, Paul was very specifically talking about the second coming. The second coming and the rapture are not the same thing at all—even rapture devotees would agree with that (well, most of them).

The other passage used as a proof text for the rapture appears in 1 Thessalonians, in which Paul writes, "Then we who are alive, who are left, will be caught up in the clouds together with them to meet the Lord in the air; and so we will be with the Lord forever" (1 Thessalonians 4:17). Now, if that were the only passage you were shown, and if you were told before reading it that it describes the rapture, *and* if you already believed that the rapture was a biblical idea: well, it's not hard to see how you would believe that this offered a definitive biblical basis for the rapture. I know I sure did. I also bought into the Latin translation argument, ignoring the fact that to get to the word *rapture*, I was using the translation of a translation that translators who are experts on translation had opted to not translate that way for very legitimate reasons, like the fact that the church had never believed in the rapture before John Darby's invention of it in the nineteenth century.

Dispensationalism's reliance on proof-texting reveals a fundamental flaw with how our modern Bibles are constructed with chapters and verses. That might sound like a strange complaint to you, but chapters and verses are a rather late addition to the Bible, not appearing as we know them today until the middle of the sixteenth century. Something like our modern chapter divisions were created a few centuries earlier, but to put all of that in context: the church went two-thirds of its life without the sort of Bible we have today.

Sure, chapters and verses can be helpful when trying to quickly look up or cite a particular passage, as I just did. But they often obscure how the books of the Bible were originally written. Most of what we call books in the New Testament weren't even books at all. They were real letters to real churches in Rome, Ephesus, Corinth, and other places around the ancient world, and just like a letter you would write today, they didn't come with chapters and verses. Just to make things even more confusing to modern readers: those letters, and the rest of the Bible, didn't even have modern sentences with punctuation and capitalization like we're accustomed to today. If you were to look at an ancient copy of, say, Paul's first letter to the church in Thessalonica, it would look like one continuous flow of words. That wouldn't have been a major issue to his original audience, because they were native speakers of the Greek language Paul was writing in.

But that sort of formatting isn't the real issue anyway. The important thing to remember when reading a letter like 1 Thessalonians is that it was originally intended to be read all at once, as one coherent thought. When we chop it up into chapters and verses and then read only a verse or two at a time, and then when we present that verse or two as definitive evidence of a claim, it's like taking one or two text messages out of a thread, or one sentence out of an entire email, and saying "This is what they meant!" But the hundreds or even thousands of words before and after that sentence could change the meaning dramatically.

The context of 1 Thessalonians 4:17 erases the possibility of this verse being a description of the rapture. We should have been tipped off by the verse itself, which begins "Then" in the NRSV and other translations—or "After that" in the NIV. If a verse begins with a transition like that, or a word like *thus* or *therefore*, it's important to ask "After what?" or "What was said before that makes this verse *therefore*?" If we zoom out a bit from 1 Thessalonians 4:17—not even to the entire letter but just to the surrounding verses—it becomes apparent fairly quickly that the "After that" matters quite a bit for understanding 1 Thessalonians 4:17. In this case, "After that" is referring to a sequence in Paul's understanding of the "coming of the Lord," or the second coming. Those who have died, or "fallen asleep" (NIV), will go first (verse 16). Then, "after that," those who are still alive will join them and Jesus and be with him forever.

But isn't that the rapture?

No.

The rapture is a moment when believers who are walking around on earth are zapped away to heaven to join Jesus there and to avoid the tribulation until Jesus returns to clean up the mess down below and start things over. What Paul is describing in 1 Thessalonians is the second coming itself. How do we know? Because Paul said Jesus is "coming down from heaven." In the rapture, Jesus stays up in heaven and we go up to meet him. Unfortunately, the key word here—*meet*—originates in Greek, not English. The word *apantesis* means "meet," but it means "meet" in a very specific way. *Apantesis* describes a visit from a dignitary. In antiquity—that is to say, in Paul's day— if a dignitary came to visit a town, some of the citizens of that town would go out to meet him as he approached. What makes this practice so important to our understanding is that the dignitary always continued on into the town. Dignitaries never just met the people they were visiting outside of town and then turned around to leave.[1] In the rapture, Jesus, the visiting dignitary, comes just above the earth, where the faithful meet him in the air before he turns around and returns to heaven with them. What Paul is describing in 1 Thessalonians is the completely opposite type of encounter. In Paul's twinkling of an eye, Jesus returns for good. He never turns around and goes back to heaven.

If we keep reading, in chapter 5 we see Paul clarify again that he is talking about "the day of the Lord"—that is, the return, or second coming, of Jesus. After his famous description of the "twinkling of an eye" in 1 Corinthians 15:52, Paul goes on to borrow from Jesus himself. Like Jesus, Paul talks about a thief in the night as he encourages the church, in the closing of his letter to the Thessalonians, to stay faithful to Jesus until he returns because Jesus will do so when they least expect it, like a thief in the night. It's a phrase Jesus used to describe his return, not the rapture.

This leads us to yet another passage that needs a bit of unrapturing: the so-called Little Apocalypse in the Gospels. In Matthew 24 we get the well-known caution from Jesus telling us that "about that day or hour no one knows, neither the angels in heaven, nor the Son, but only the Father" (Matthew 24:36). Of course, even though it came from the lips of Jesus himself, that passage has never stopped dispensationalists from predicting either the rapture or the second coming. Matthew 24 is also where we get a list of the signs of the times, imagery for movies like *Thief in the Night* and lyrical inspiration for songs like the Larry Norman classic "I Wish We'd All Been Ready." Both derive from Jesus' descriptions of his return: like a thief who comes unexpectedly in the night to take everything you have, or like people working in a field or women working a hand mill, with one being taken and the other being left behind.

Two interesting things are going on here, though—things that throw a wet blanket on this passage's use as a proof text for the rapture. The first we've already talked about. Despite the beautiful harmonies of Larry Norman, it's actually not entirely clear that being left behind is a bad thing in this passage. The Greek words the writer of Matthew uses for "taken" and "left" can be used in both positive and negative ways.[2] If, for example, a hostile alien force invaded Earth, kidnapping random people and taking them away to become slaves in the spice mines of Kessel, you wouldn't want to be taken by the aliens. You would *want* to be left behind. In other words, being left behind might actually be a good thing! In fact, as we'll see later on, being left behind might even be a calling.

The subsequent chapter of Matthew's Little Apocalypse also makes it clear that Jesus is talking about his return, not a temporary visit. We know that because, in Matthew 25, Jesus continues describing both his return and how to be prepared for it, but then goes on to explain why there is such urgency to being prepared. It's not for fear of being left behind to suffer through seven years of tribulation, but because "when the Son of Man comes in his glory, and all the angels with him, then he will sit on his throne of glory" and begin the final judgment when he will divide the sheep from the goats (Matthew 25:31-33). So, while the Little Apocalypse of Matthew does make for classic rapture music, it is clear that nearly every verse is describing just one return of Jesus, not a two-stage process beginning with the rapture.

What *is* in the Bible

But the biblical problems with the rapture go much deeper than a lack of the word itself or misinterpreting proof texts. The very concept of the rapture goes against the entire narrative of the Bible—in particular, how the people of God confront trials and tribulation.

Just take a look at some of the major characters in Scripture. Very few, if any, had anything resembling what we would call an easy or good life. Sure, there were good times here and there. Eden was literally paradise, the Promised Land flowed with milk and honey, and after his epic trial, Job was blessed with riches far greater than he had before. But if it is nothing else, the story of the Bible is a sustained narrative of how God sees God's people through trials and tribulations, not how God whisks them away to safety before the trials and tribulations begin.

God warned Noah that a flood is coming and told him to build a boat to protect his family, but the ark was no pleasure cruise. Noah and his family were trapped inside a dark, dirty, stinky ark with a menagerie of animals for months on end, after listening to their neighbors beat against the walls of the ark until they all drowned and everything and everyone Noah and his family had ever known had been utterly destroyed. The story of Noah's ark isn't a fairy tale of God whisking God's people away from trials and tribulations. It's a horror story of the most unimaginable kind.

God called Abraham and promised to bless him and make of him a great nation, but Abraham's journey was anything but easy. He had to leave his friends and homeland behind. He almost lost his wife in Egypt. He did lose his nephew and his family. He almost lost his son. There was family drama with ripple effects that carry on all the way to the present day. Abraham may have been blessed, but God didn't whisk him away from trials and tribulations. The same was true for Abraham's descendants.

Abraham's great-grandson Joseph was sold into slavery by his brothers. The great nation that Abraham's faithfulness gave birth to spent four hundred years in slavery. Israel's liberator,

Moses, was constantly berated by the people of Israel and riddled with doubt while wandering in the wilderness with them
for four decades. Life in the Promised Land saw a never-ending
succession of evil and corrupt kings. Despite a life of faithful
devotion, Job lost his entire family and everything he had. The
people of Israel were eventually conquered and shipped off in
bondage to Babylon.

Even Jesus didn't escape brutal trials and tribulation. Pursued by Herod as a baby, he and his family became refugees.
When he grew up, he was an outcast in his own hometown.
His ministry culminated in being betrayed by one of his best
friends and then being arrested, tried, publicly humiliated,
beaten, flogged, spit on, stripped naked, and nailed to a cross.
Yes, Jesus rose triumphantly from the grave, defeated death,
and changed the course of history through the power of his
resurrection. But that wasn't the end of trials and tribulations
for his disciples. Jesus' followers constantly faced persecution
and even infighting within the church. Very few of them were
not martyred. Tradition says Peter was crucified upside down
and Paul was executed by the very Roman government to
which he appealed for mercy.

So the idea of a rapture, in which God whisks God's people away to safety and away from people who need our help,
isn't just nonbiblical; it's *anti*-biblical. And when we consider
the incarnation itself—that God didn't stay up in heaven but
came down to earth to dwell among us and all the problems
we create—the rapture becomes more than just not biblical. It
becomes antichrist.

No, not the guy from the Left Behind series. I mean antichrist in the sense of being antithetical to the way of Christ,
the way of Jesus.

The way of Jesus

Lack of biblical support not withstanding, this is the fundamental problem with the rapture and the end-times theology
that goes with it: it creates a way of life that stands in stark
juxtaposition to the way of Jesus. The way of Jesus is incarnation, but the way of the rapture is escape. Jesus came to bring
the kingdom of God down to earth as it is in heaven, but end-
times theology seeks to leave earth and its problems behind.
Jesus was born in human flesh because God cares about the
here and now. Jesus went out across Galilee because God cares
about the here and now. Jesus called disciples and taught them
how to live because God cares about the here and now. Jesus
healed and fed people because God cares about the here and
now. Jesus laid down his life because God cares about the
here and now. Jesus rose from the dead, leaving behind the
gift of the Spirit and promising to come back here to earth,
because God cares about the here and now. The way of Jesus
is incarnation in the here and now—not escape to some far-off
safe place.

The rapture promises we can leave the world behind, creating a radically self-centered faith that is all about me and how
I get to heaven and avoid going to hell. The rapture makes discipleship irrelevant because all it takes to escape hell on earth
and hell down below is belief in the right things. Jesus calls us
to be his hands and feet in the here and now, but end-times
theology, with the rapture at its center, tells us to sit around
and wait for God to act.

This problematic foundation leads us to a long list of very
specific here-and-now problems that the rapture and end-times
theology create beyond just bad exegesis and poor discipleship.
It all starts with a nation that seems so very biblical: Israel.

Israel's role in end-times theology

Whether it's Jack Van Impe, the Left Behind series, Hal Lindsey, or any other self-proclaimed expert, end-times theology
begins, ends, and is driven along the way by Israel. Israel-
related news usually manages to get spun by dispensationalists
into some sort of prophecy fulfillment or precursor to prophecy fulfillment. The establishment of the modern state of Israel
in 1948? Prophecy. The Six-Day War? Prophecy. The Oslo
Accords? Prophecy. Donald Trump moving the U.S. embassy
to Jerusalem? Prophecy.[3]

If dispensationalists were just spinning old news to fit their
end-times chronologies, that would be one thing. But they're
also driving foreign policy in the United States and giving cover
to the nation of Israel for anything it does. For example, Jack
Van Impe claimed to have been consulted by the national security advisor during the George W. Bush administration to see
how then-current events in the Middle East lined up with biblical prophecy.[4] For years, in a move the international community has denounced as illegal, the state of Israel has stolen land
from Palestinians under the euphemism of "settlements." In
the process, Israel has committed all sorts of atrocities against
Palestinian civilians, even turning Bethlehem, the birthplace
of Jesus, into a de facto prison through the construction of
a wall that restricts access for outsiders and limits travel for
residents. All of this is defended in the United States by people
on both sides of the aisle and for a variety of reasons. But
arguably Israel's most staunch defender in the United States is
the Republican Party, which is driven by an evangelical base
that excuses all of Israel's actions as part of reclaiming the
land promised to them by God in the Bible. In other words, in
the world of dispensationalism, what we are witnessing is not

the political defense of another nation-state. It's the fulfillment of biblical prophecy.

President Trump, in an action clearly meant to appeal to the 81 percent of white evangelicals who voted for him, moved the U.S. embassy from Tel Aviv to Jerusalem. This action was met not just with international condemnation but with violent protests that resulted in the deaths of nearly sixty people.[5] But again, dispensationalists saw Trump's decision as a fulfillment of Scripture—even though there is no such prophecy in the Bible or anywhere else in the Christian tradition. As for the dozens of people who died? They were just collateral damage, unavoidable sacrifices to the cause of biblical prophecy.

Beyond the issue of occupation, there are at least three other significant problems with this Israel-driven prophetic agenda. The first is that the modern nation-state of Israel is not the same Israel as in the Bible. This is one of the most basic mistakes that dispensationalists make. They conflate the people of God in the Bible with a modern political state. They are not the same. One was established by God when he called Abraham to leave his homeland—a promise fulfilled generations later when Moses led the people of Israel (the name of Abraham's grandson) out of Egypt and eventually to the Promised Land. The modern state of Israel was declared after the partition of Palestine into Jewish and Arab states by the United Nations after World War II.

Secondly, the biblical prophecies that Jack Van Impe and others breathlessly claim are being fulfilled in the Middle East are a lot like the rapture: that is, they're not actually biblical. There is no passage in Revelation, Daniel, Matthew, or anywhere else in the Bible that says X, Y, or Z must happen in Israel in order for Jesus to return. What we see are dispensationalists taking real events as they unfold, contorting them to fit their predetermined maps and timelines, and then finding proof texts in the Bible to back up their claims.

Finally, and most importantly, is the aforementioned problem of sanctified violence. Yes, both Palestine and Israel are committing violent actions in the battle for control of what they both view as their homeland. But conspicuously, the only side ever condemned by dispensationalists, conservative evangelicals, and even the U.S. government is the Palestinians. They are perpetually cast as the bad guys standing in the way of Israel's divine right to the land and therefore, somehow, preventing the return of Jesus. Yes, there is violence and guilt on the Palestinian side as well, but dispensationalism never holds Israel accountable for indefensible acts of violence against innocent men, women, and children, or for the theft and destruction of Palestinian homes and land. It is all sanctified in the name of fulfilling biblical prophecy. Dispensationalists who have decided that all Palestinians are their enemies rarely if ever stop to consider the fact that many Palestinians are Christians too.

This leads us to yet another core problem with end-times theology: its Machiavellian ethics.

Ethics suspended

The basic idea behind dispensationalism is that there are different time periods, or dispensations, throughout history. According to dispensationalists, we are living right before the final dispensation when Jesus will return and establish his kingdom on earth. This sounds nice and good until you flip the coin over and see the other side. The underbelly of dispensationalism is its Machiavellian "ends justify the means" theology. Because we are supposedly living before the final dispensation, and because we must do everything we can to make sure biblical prophecy is fulfilled so Jesus can return, normal ethics are suspended for the sake of the cause. With a moratorium on morality, dispensationalist Christians free themselves to turn a blind eye toward a whole host of atrocities not just in Israel but also here at home because, tragic as those atrocities might be, they can always be justified in the name of biblical prophecy.

Ironically, this is the very thing that conservative Christianity warned me about when I was growing up. Whether it was in church, at a big youth event, or on *Jack Van Impe Presents*, I was constantly warned about the dangers of moral relativism—how the godless liberals were taking over and forcing moral relativism onto everyone to make way for the Antichrist. Christians, I was told, must stand firm in their convictions and values no matter what. But that edict was suddenly, if subtly, suspended whenever biblical prophecy was at stake. Whenever biblical prophecy was at stake, moral relativism suddenly stopped being the evil boogeyman and became the movement of the Holy Spirit.

A prime example of this is the 2016 election of Donald Trump as president of the United States. Trump is a known adulterer, liar, cheat, and gambler, a thrice-divorced, unapologetically crass, immoral, racist business mogul who uses fearmongering to rile up the worst in people while refusing to apologize for anything he's done. On paper, he's the kind of person who should make evangelical Christians reel back in horror. But 81 percent of white evangelical voters supported him, and despite a never-ending wave of scandals, racism, and bigotry since the election, that number has barely budged.[6]

White evangelical support for Trump is rooted in many realities, including radical partisanship, economic anxiety, racism, and a desire to overturn *Roe v. Wade*. But end-times theology can't be overlooked as an important force in their embrace of him as a presidential candidate. If you tuned in to any pro-Trump Christian media outlet during the election or since, you would hear his Christian supporters describe him in the terms of a biblical king—even a pagan biblical king like the Babylonian king Cyrus, placed or chosen by God and anointed as God's chosen leader for "such a time as this" (Esther 4:14). Ironically, it was Esther, not Cyrus, whom God anointed for "such a time as this," to use her position to bring justice to those being oppressed and marginalized by their government, but awkward details are easily and often ignored in the world of biblical prophecy.[7]

From his promise to overturn *Roe v. Wade* to his over-the-top support for Israel to his guarantee that clerks at Target will say "Merry Christmas," Trump is viewed by many of his Christian supporters as a fulfillment of biblical prophecy. It's why they can not only look past but even justify his countless sins. We are on the brink of the final dispensation, they believe, and to make it over that brink, we must do whatever is necessary. Otherwise Jesus won't be able to return, because prophecy will not have been fulfilled. The suspension of ethics is necessary to ensure the fulfillment of those prophecies, because that fulfillment can sometimes be nasty business, like chasing Palestinians off their land or waging war on the Muslim world to take back the Temple Mount. The end, which is the fulfillment of biblical prophecy and the second coming of Jesus, justifies the means, which is electing someone like Donald Trump. If his election means the fulfillment of key prophecies on the dispensationalist timeline, then we should overlook the unsavory details.

Trump also embodies another underlying problem that is, ironically, also incredibly appealing to many who believe in the rapture and the tribulation that follows: vengeance against one's enemies.

Donald Trump is notorious for holding a grudge, for punching down and attacking anyone for even the most minuscule slight. He trashes his enemies, both real and perceived, on a daily basis and promises to wipe them off the face of the earth with fire and fury. In some ways, he is the incarnation of a dispensationalist Savior. For dispensationalism, the Savior we see in Revelation fixes the "mistakes" Jesus made in the Gospels: his soft stance on sin and crime, all that mushy stuff about loving our enemies, and most importantly, his humiliating defeat on the cross. A dispensational Savior returns to crush his enemies and wipe them off the face of the earth once and for all. But first, faithful Christians get to be zapped up to heaven, where they'll have a front row seat to revenge as they witness their enemies tortured and killed during the seven years of the tribulation.

Vengeance might not be the first thing that comes to mind when you think about the rapture or the end times, but consider what dispensationalism is really promising, with its talk of things like the rapture, the tribulation, and Armageddon. When the rapture happens, their smug enemies will be left behind and ashamed, forever having to face the truth that they were wrong and the Christians were right. But that's just the beginning of their apocalyptic nightmare. The tribulation isn't just a period of time without the benefit of nice Christians around to say "Have a blessed day" when you pull away from

Chick-fil-A. The tribulation is a time when all the unbelievers left behind—all the enemies of the Christians that were raptured—are tortured for seven years through a series of plagues, wars, and all sorts of Antichrist-directed violence.

After the tribulation ends, there's still more violence. After the tribulation comes Armageddon, the actual "war to end all wars." It's a massacre of unprecedented proportions, in which the enemies of God (or more accurately, enemies of dispensationalist Christians) will finally get their comeuppance. But even Armageddon is still not the end of dispensational vengeance. Once the hell of the tribulation and Armageddon is over, there's still actual hell to deal with. In the timeline of dispensationalism, everyone, whether they've been raptured or left behind, will be dragged before the judgment seat to face the music. Their entire lifetime's worth of sins will be read in excruciating detail for all of humanity to hear, and then Jesus will send all the unrepentant people to hell, where they will be tortured for eternity.

So when dispensationalists sanctify violence in the Middle East, atrocities by the state of Israel, or hatred, violence, and vitriol from Donald Trump, they can spin it as living out biblical prophecy, as a prophetic act of affirming the truth of what is to come by living it out in the here and now. It's like a perverse eucharist. It's living out the promise of the future here in the present, but in an objectively un-Christlike way. Yet violence is not seen as antichrist in end-times theology. It is the way of dispensationalist Jesus. It's how dispensationalist Jesus is going to make the world right again. And because Jesus is coming back, enemies aren't the only ones who suffer the wrath of end-times theology.

The earth does too.

New heaven, new earth

At the heart of the incarnation-versus-escape dynamic is the issue of climate change. In the beginning, God commanded Adam and Eve to care for the creation God had given them— care for, not exploit. The word *dominion* often appears in our English Bibles, but the Hebrew word being translated as "dominion" (*radah*) isn't about exploitation. *Radah* is the sort of responsibility Old Testament kings were called to have. The kings of Israel weren't anointed by God to exploit their subjects however they saw fit. They were called to care for the people of Israel by ensuring justice for the poor and defending the weak. In the same way, the call of Genesis to have "dominion" over the earth is a call to care for the earth, not exploit it for our own selfish ends. We've obviously not done a great job of that task to steward the earth, and as a result, the climate is changing rapidly. Temperatures are rising, and sea levels with them. Glaciers are disappearing and so are animal species and entire ways of life for people in coastal communities.[8]

As caretakers of the garden—people with a divine calling to care for creation—we should be at the forefront of caring for creation. But we're not. In fact, the very idea of climate change is anathema to many American Christians, particularly dispensationalists. Part of the refusal to accept the truth about climate change is the result of a never-ending stream of propaganda from right-wing media. The years-long effort to brainwash people on behalf of the oil and gas industries can't be overstated. But when we talk about the church and climate change, we cannot overlook the role that dispensationalism plays in neglecting creation.

When most of us read the last two chapters of Revelation and hear about a new heaven and new earth, where there will be no more sickness or death or sorrow or mourning, for the old things will have passed away and all things will be made new—when we read that, our hearts are warmed and our souls are filled with hope. That's true for dispensationalists as well. But end-times theology also gives them a pass—a "get out of jail free" card—for caring about the environment. After all, why do we need to make sure our oceans are clean and the air is breathable if Jesus is just going to set it all on fire and start over again?

While climate change denial might be new, escapism and ambivalence are not. They've been around as long as Revelation itself. In the sixteenth century, long before fossil fuels were invented or factories were chugging out smoke, the famous reformer Martin Luther is said to have confronted this attitude directly. What was his apocryphal response to a laissez-faire attitude about caring about the here and now if Jesus is just going to start everything over again? "Even if I knew the world would end tomorrow, I would plant a tree." It's a defiant statement, one that speaks to our call to incarnate faith in the here and how. But it also hints at the fact that a new heaven and a new earth is about renewal of what we have here. God isn't starting over from scratch. This is why Paul said the form of this world is passing away, not the world itself (1 Corinthians 7:31). Think of it in terms of the resurrection. When Jesus was raised from the dead, he was raised in a glorified body, but it was still the same body that had hung on the cross. His hands still had holes from the nails, his forehead scars from the crown of thorns, and his side gashes from the spears.

We have to take care of the earth because this is the only one we have, because God has called us to do so, and because this is the one God will be renewing, not re-creating. Our job as God's hands and feet in the world is to begin that renewal in the here and now, not to wait for God to do it at some unknown point in the future. Creation care is an act of resurrection, the firstfruits of the final restoration that is to come. It restores to life what we've destroyed, and in doing so, lays the groundwork for Christ's return, when God will bring to completion the work begun in the garden of Eden.

This brings us back to the fundamental problem with the rapture: it calls us to escape, while Jesus calls us to incarnation. The rapture calls us to look only at ourselves, while Jesus calls us to die to self and live our lives for others. For all the rapture's focus on going off to heaven to live with Jesus forever, the life it calls us to lead in the here and now is, at its very core, antichrist.

7

Undragoning

Blood was dripping slowly but steadily from my thumb as if it were a water balloon that had sprung a leak. As it ran out of real estate on my hand, it began to cascade down to the ground, staining the green Florida turf a dark crimson red. But I didn't notice. It wasn't until someone tapped me on the shoulder and said "Uh, Zack, I think you're bleeding" that I looked down and saw the horror show unfolding beneath the blazing summer sun.

In my rush to open up a can of tomatoes, I forgot that I am utterly incapable of multitasking. So when a group of kids at the church camp I was working at started asking me questions about a game being played on the field next to us, I took my eyes off the can. It slipped in my sweat-drenched hand and sliced a deep gash in my thumb. The other counselors were urging me to go see the camp nurse, but there was no time for that. I had to get the tomatoes into the kiddie pool for Tomato Bobbing, check on the plates of old spaghetti for the Clean the Plate relay race, and make sure the cartons of eggs were ready to go for Raw Egg Ultimate Frisbee. The Gross Games Olympics were my baby, and there was no way I was going to let them fail. The show had to go on, whether or not I had a thumb. Some things are just more important than appendages.

You see, a few months earlier, my former youth pastor Tony, who at the time was working in the admissions department at Trevecca, approached me on campus one day about joining what the school called the Summer Ministry Team. Essentially, it was a public relations group that would help bring attention to the school across the Church of the Nazarene's southeast region. In practice that meant traveling around to district teen camps, where we would lead worship and recreation, and hopefully convince a few kids to go to Trevecca. At first I told Tony I had changed my mind about going into youth ministry. The passion I once had for ministry had evaporated with my faith in the rapture. I was too bitter about my misplaced faith to care about the faith of others. But he didn't give up, perhaps because he had been there when I first felt called to ministry and had let me job shadow him. Maybe he thought spending the summer working with teenagers at summer camps was the thing I needed to rediscover my passionate call to ministry. Or maybe he was just desperate for help. Either way, I wasn't convinced until he mentioned there was a paycheck and free Chick-fil-A involved. Miraculously, I felt the Spirit calling me again.

I went into that summer trying to have an open mind about considering youth ministry again. College was ending soon, and my only training was in ministry—well, that and a few law classes, but one practice LSAT was enough to scare me away from law school. So a summer hanging out with teenagers it was. Maybe I would at least make a few connections that could lead to a youth ministry job, and thus a paycheck, while I figured out what I really wanted to do with my life.

Bags packed, I hopped into a white fifteen-passenger van with the other members of the Summer Ministry Team, and we hit the open road. My job was to lead recreation at the different camps and occasionally fill in playing the guitar with the worship band when our regular guitar player couldn't make the trip. We traveled all over the southeastern United States, from Tennessee to Florida, leading worship, playing elaborate games we wished we had played when we were in youth group, and promoting Trevecca with free swag.

I had a blast. For the first time in a long time, I felt that I was doing what I was meant to do. I don't mean leading games and playing the guitar; I mean all the moments in between, getting to know the teenagers we were working with at the camps. Listening to them imagine what college was going to be like, sharing a laugh as they gave each other grief after an epic game of kickball, and being a shoulder to cry on when the boy or girl they were absolutely, positively in love with now and forever didn't feel quite the same way.

I discovered that summer that I really did love working with teenagers. Positive reinforcement from youth pastors at the camps we worked at encouraged me to rethink my call to ministry. Slowly but surely, I began to realize that maybe ministry wasn't a punishment for changing worship songs into fart songs as a kid. Nor was it a way to feel spiritually superior to others while scaring them into heaven. Maybe ministry was actually an invitation to join God in doing amazing things in the lives of others.

What I thought would just be a summer of free food and paid travel had suddenly become a time of confirmation of my call to ministry. The summer after I graduated from college, Tony invited me and another member of the Summer Ministry Team on another adventure, this time to intern at the church where Tony was now serving as youth pastor. It was in the small and swelteringly hot town of Venice, Florida.

The big thing Venice does have going for it is its proximity to the beach. The church where I worked was just a mile or two from the ocean. In my head I thought I would be spending my entire summer lounging on the beach when I wasn't hanging out with teenagers at church. Want to guess how many times I went to the beach that summer? Once. Not because the beach in Venice isn't great. It is. I hear you can find shark teeth in the surf. But living at the beach is nothing like vacationing at the beach. You actually have to go to work and do all the other things that come with regular, boring, everyday life, like going grocery shopping, cleaning your house, getting your oil changed, yada yada yada.

Plus, going to the beach means going outside, and just going outside in the south Florida summer is a chore in itself. The humidity is unbearable. And I say that as someone born and raised in the South. It gets uncomfortably hot and humid in my home state of Tennessee, but south Florida is literally a swamp. In the summer, the swamp earns its reputation as an inhospitable wasteland. Forget trying to save money on electricity by leaving your windows open. You've got to keep those things sealed shut and crank the AC as high as it'll go; otherwise you'll die. Probably. I can't say for sure, as we never risked it.

One afternoon, on our quest to stay wrapped up in the sweet embrace of ice-cold air conditioning, Tony, the other intern, and I found ourselves wandering around a small

Christian bookstore. To be fair, we probably would have done that regardless of the weather. We were pastors and pastors in training, and pastors and pastors in training like spending afternoons in Christian bookstores. So there we were, soaking up the air conditioning and finding something to spend our humble intern checks on.

After wandering aimlessly, taking books off the shelves, reading the back covers, and putting them back on the shelf, I was beginning to run out of books to look at. But then I found my eyes drawn to a small yellow book with red typeface on the lowest shelf. The artwork looked interesting, so I picked it up to get a better look. It was titled *Pocket Guide to the Apocalypse: The Official Field Manual for the End of the World*, by Jason Boyett. I had no clue who Jason Boyett was, but the title was catchy.[1] So I started thumbing through it.

It was unlike anything I had ever seen in a Christian bookstore before. It was hilarious. Way funnier than it should have been, hidden away on a humble bottom shelf in a random bookstore in a retirement community. The endorsement alone deserved some sort of award: "This guy is gonna be so left behind. —Jerry Jenkins"

That would be *the* Jerry Jenkins, as in coauthor of the Left Behind series Jerry Jenkins. Obviously it was tongue in cheek, but the faux endorsement worked. I bought the book immediately and rushed home to read it.

The book was exactly as described: a small pocket-sized guide to all things end times. There was a chapter on the origins of end-times theology, a glossary of important end-times terms and ideas, a chapter chronicling all the failed predictions of Jesus' return, a list of potential candidates for the Antichrist (according to self-proclaimed experts), and much, much more.

While there was tons of great information such as you might find in a textbook, it was all done in a hilarious, tongue-in-cheek sort of way. I loved it for what it was: a clever approach to an often murky and controversial subject. But what I loved even more was what it did for me.

It gave me permission to laugh at myself.

I was only three years removed from being the sort of person who could have had his own entry in the rogues' gallery of failed rapture predictions. I was finally coming to grips with how wrong I had been and only starting the process of rebuilding my faith. I was still deeply embarrassed by my apocalyptic past. The *Pocket Guide* poked good-natured fun at people like me, or at least people like I had been. It wasn't an attack. It let me put my guard down and see how not alone I was in my arrogance.

It wasn't an instantaneous revelation. My defenses were still strong, and it took a while for me to recognize that the person I was laughing at in that book was myself. Even then, it took still more time to let go of the embarrassment. But once I did, I didn't find humiliation; I found liberation. The chains of dogmatism and the need to be right fell off. I felt theologically free for the first time, maybe ever.

But it wasn't an easy process. In fact, it was often quite painful. Still is. I'm nowhere near being done learning to have the humility I need.

Dragonhide

When my faith got unraptured, it wasn't a humbling experience so much as a humiliating and painful one. It was kind of like what Eustace goes through in C. S. Lewis's *The Voyage of the Dawn Treader*. Eustace is a spoiled, know-it-all self-centered brat when he lands with his cousins in the magical land of Narnia, and he finds himself magically transformed into a dragon. It's a transformation that eventually sees his character transformed as well. But the transformation process isn't easy, painless, or one he can do alone.

While hiding from his fellow travelers so as not to burden them with the decision of whether to leave him behind (since as a dragon he can't fit back on their boat), Eustace meets the great lion, Aslan. Aslan, the Christ figure in the Narnia series, has the power to transform Eustace back into a boy, but it won't be easy. Aslan tells him he can enter a pool of healing water, but first he has to get undressed—a command that confuses Eustace, who is still a dragon and thus not wearing any clothes. It eventually dawns on Eustace that dragons are snakelike creatures, and that snakes can shed their skin. So he begins to scratch at his dragon scales until they all fall off. But he still can't enter the healing waters, because Aslan tells him that he still needs to undress. Once again Eustace stands befuddled, thinking he has done what was asked of him, and yet there is somehow still more work to do. Eventually he begins to claw at his raw, scaleless skin. It is incredibly painful, but he keeps going because he's desperate to be healed.

Unfortunately for Eustace, it turns out that he *still* has not removed enough of his old self to enter the healing waters. What remains—the raw core of who he is—is something only Aslan can remove. And he does, tearing the last bit of dragon flesh away from Eustace with his great lion claws. It is an excruciating process but a necessary one—one that fully opens up Eustace to the healing power of the water, which he is finally able to enter. Stripped fully of his old self, he can be healed and made new. Stripped of his arrogance and self-centeredness, he finds himself welcomed back into community by those who never rejected him but whom he could never before embrace as equals.

As a child, I never gave much thought to the undragoning of Eustace. If it hurt, I thought back then, he was just getting what he deserved for being such an insufferable pain to others. I now realize that I was Eustace. Clothed in a thick hide of dragon skin built up over years of memorizing Bible verses, studying prophetic charts, learning airtight theological defenses, surrounding myself only with Christian people, listening only to Christian music, and wearing only Christian clothes—donned in my spiritual armor, I thought myself invincible, a devastating force of destruction should anyone dare try to tell me I was wrong about anything. I had the dragonhide of Christ and couldn't be stopped.

But unlike Eustace, I didn't have the wisdom or courage to start peeling off my arrogant exterior. I had to have it ripped off for me. But it didn't come off quickly like a cheap Band-Aid. What started in my professor's office that day in college took years to see through, and it still hasn't reached completion. My faith may be more open and inclusive now, but real Christlike humility often remains elusive. Thankfully, though, humility is no longer something I see as the Achilles heel of the spiritually weak.

That day in my professor's office and the years that followed did teach me one thing: how much I don't know. That's the ironic thing about learning. The more you know, the more you realize how much you don't know. Properly done, learning should make us more humble, not less. It should open our eyes to our own finitude, and when done in the context of faith, learning has the power to reveal the beauty of the divine at work in ways and places and people we never thought possible.

I still have a long way to go, but learning how much I don't know may be the most important lesson I've ever learned. It broke me away from the pathology of fundamentalism: an arrogant need to be right about everything. More importantly, it allowed me to look at the Bible with new eyes and embrace its mysteries and complexities without trying to reconcile and fix everything so that it all fit neatly inside my theological box.

But I didn't do it alone. I had two guides in my quest to become undragoned—two saints of the church who helped me recover the Bible from dispensationalism and the weaponization of Scripture I thought was the way of the righteous. These guides helped me better understand the Bible and, more specifically, Revelation and the end times, and to see them in a whole new light. Their names were Origen and Augustine, and they died long before Jack Van Impe arrived on the scene.

Help from a heretic

Origen was one of the earliest and most influential of the church fathers and mothers. The reason you may not be familiar with him is the sad fact that in the year 553 CE, long after his death in 253 CE, his teachings—or to be more precise, teachings espoused much later by a group who self-connected to Origen—were declared heretical. But before Origen was unjustly condemned as a heretic, he wrote one of the most important works in the history of the church: *De Principiis*, or *On First Principles*. It was a passage in that book that, along with the work of Origen's theological heir Saint Augustine, forever changed how I read and understand the Bible, especially a mysterious book like Revelation.

Origen believed there are two senses in Scripture: the literal and the spiritual. The literal is, as it sounds, the words that are literally written on the page. This is how dispensationalists approach the book of Revelation. They read it as a literal rather than metaphorical or symbolic account of the future. This is why the Left Behind series found such a welcome embrace: it fleshes out a literal reading of Revelation in a way that readers said makes the Bible come alive.[2]

Unfortunately, a literal reading of the Bible is also what allows fundamentalism to turn the Bible into a weapon. A so-called plain reading of the Bible is used to transform countless context-free verses into weapons against any number of "sinners." It can sound convincing on the surface, this idea that the righteous warrior isn't being judgmental or cruel, they're simply quoting what the Bible clearly says. But "a plain reading of the Bible" is anything but. The only thing plain about it is the literal way in which it reads every weaponized verse without any attempt to understand the context, both immediately within a particular chapter or book and in the wider context of the gospel. Even in a plain reading, interpretation is still going on. In using a verse out of context and saying "*This* is what is meant," we are interpreting that verse's meaning. Which is why a plain reading of the Bible is anything but plain.

While there are certainly moments in the Bible when the literal words on the page are what God wants us to hear, pretending as if every sentence in the Bible should be read without context and then followed literally has led to all sorts of atrocities committed in the name of God. From the Crusades and slavery to Jim Crow and the treatment of the LGBT community, proof-texting the Bible under the auspices of a plain or literal reading too often leads us to proclaiming the very opposite of good news.

We forget that the Bible didn't drop from heaven. Inspired by God, the words of the Bible were written by human beings, human beings whose own biases, prejudices, cultural context, and historical ignorance sometimes got in the way of the good news. It's something Paul himself acknowledged in his second letter to Timothy when he writes, "All Scripture is God-breathed and is useful for teaching, rebuking, correcting and training in righteousness" (2 Timothy 3:16 NIV). It's a powerful passage confirming the authority of Scripture. But what exactly does "God-breathed" mean? A linguistic analysis of the original Greek isn't a ton of help here; *God-breathed* is simply the English translation of the Greek work *theópneustos*. But as it always does, context can give us a clue about what it means for something to be God-breathed. To find that contextual clue, we have to zoom out from the immediate verse, out from Paul's letter, and out from the New Testament entirely. There is only one other passage in the entire Bible in which something is described as being God-breathed.

It's found in the very beginning of a book that would have been foundational to Paul's theology: the book of Genesis. In the story of creation, it's on the sixth day that God takes the dust of the earth and breathes into it the breath of life. In other words, humanity is God-breathed. And yet . . . we're not perfect. If we were, we would simply *be* God or, at the very least, a bunch of little gods. But we're not perfect; we're God-breathed, not God-incarnated. God-breathed doesn't mean perfection, because God doesn't take over our lives and control us like puppets. God gives us free will so that we can have a real relationship with God; that free will means we can and do choose to do imperfect things.

Scripture is God-breathed, writes Paul. As part of the relationship God has invited us to participate in, we help in the work of reconciling all of creation back to its Creator. The Bible is part of that work. The Bible functions both as a guide toward reconciliation and as a testimony to how that work has already begun. That work of participating in reconciliation doesn't require perfection on our part. It simply requires a willingness to try. It's God's perfecting grace that brings to completion the reconciliation of creation to its Creator. We'll stumble and fall and get some things wrong along the way, but as long as we keep pointing people in the right direction by loving one another as God first loved us, the Holy Spirit will take care of the rest. That's why it doesn't matter if there are contradictions in Scripture. They don't affect our ability to tell the core truths about God. They're simply the natural result of the Bible being written by imperfect people.

Origen embraced the flaws of the biblical writers because in them, he saw God using human imperfection to draw us closer to God by challenging us to think harder about what it truly means to follow God. Origen had a name for such imperfections; he called them "stumbling blocks." He said the Holy Spirit allowed them to be in Scripture not to mislead or trick us but to force us to wrestle with what is being said, much like the writers of Scripture themselves must have wrestled with how best to communicate the message God had placed on their hearts. In confronting the "stumbling blocks" of Scripture in this way, Origen argued, we are drawn deeper into the text—past the literal words on the page and toward what he called the "spiritual sense" of

Scripture. This is where God wants us to be; this is where the truth of Scripture lies.

As Origen explains, this spiritual sense is

kept hidden and covered in the narratives of holy Scripture, because "the kingdom of heaven is like a treasure hid in a field; which when a man findeth, he hideth it, and for joy thereof goeth away and selleth all that he hath, and buyeth that field." By which similitude, consider whether it be not pointed out that the very soil and surface, so to speak, of Scripture—that is, the literal meaning—is the field, filled with plants and flowers of all kinds; while that deeper and profounder "spiritual" meaning are the very hidden treasures of wisdom and knowledge which the Holy Spirit by Isaiah calls the dark and invisible and hidden treasures, for the finding out of which the divine help is required.[3]

In other words, Origen would say it is impossible to simply open up our Bibles, turn to a random page, and perfectly understand the message God is trying to communicate to us. The mysteries of the faith can't be unraveled on a whim, nor can the complexities of life be uncomplicated with a proof text. Reading and interpreting not only takes hard work; it also requires the work of the Holy Spirit, which is often more mundane than it is mystical.

One of the great gifts of the Holy Spirit is wisdom and understanding. But too often we smugly dismiss the work of biblical scholars as nothing more than esoteric ranting of cynics in the ivory tower who want to tear apart our faith. Too rarely do we stop to consider that perhaps biblical scholars are doing the work of the Spirit, that their wisdom and understanding of the Bible comes from the Holy Spirit who is working through them to help us better understand Scripture. Too often we miss the movement and inspiration of the Holy

Spirit because we relegate the Spirit to the supernatural and don't allow for God to work in the mundane. We want God to speak to us through a burning bush, when more often than not God is revealing the truth of Scripture to us through a biblical commentary. If the Bible is full of hidden treasure, we need people proficient in biblical mining to help us know where and how to dig down deep to find those scriptural treasures. We need them to help us know when we've actually stumbled upon treasure and when we've just found fool's gold.

There are few greater examples than the book of Revelation of Scripture that needs deep digging to find the hidden truth. It's a book cloaked in the mystery of apocalyptic language and set in a time far removed from our own. As we've seen, to read that language literally not only misses the deeper spiritual truth that is being conveyed; it creates a whole host of earthly problems as well. A literal reading of Revelation allows Palestinians to be oppressed, violence to be condoned, and morality to be suspended in the pursuit of fulfilling what dispensationalism claims is the literal meaning of John's apocalypse. Dispensationalism claims to have deciphered the deeper spiritual meaning of Scripture, but more often than not, it uses the literal words on the page to sanctify ways of being in the world that go against the name and character of Christ.

But this phenomenon is far more widespread than Revelation. The underlying problem with a dispensationalist approach to Scripture is the same as any approach that uses biblical proof texts to justify unloving things in the name of God. When taken literally and out of context, Scripture meant to liberate and redeem can instead be used to afflict, marginalize, and oppress our enemies. We desperately need a better way to read the Bible in general and Revelation in particular, especially now that a literal reading has become a driving force in the political life of the church.

So how do we do that? How do we know when to dig deeper into Scripture? How do we know when to search beyond the literal meaning to find the spiritual truth God wants us to hear? And when we search, how do we know what we should be looking for and what reading of the text is inspired by God? To begin to answer those questions, we need to turn to another church father, Saint Augustine.

Augustine and the greatest commandment

Born in the middle of the fourth century in what is now the African nation of Algeria to a pagan father and a Christian mother, Saint Augustine of Hippo has had more influence on Western theology than any other church father. He was a prolific writer and staunch defender of Christian orthodoxy, penning such influential works as *Confessions*, *City of God*, and *On the Trinity*.

Augustine wrote another text that sounds almost as if he had just finished reading Origen when he wrote it. In *The Literal Meaning of Genesis*, Augustine—writing fifteen hundred years before Darwin's theory of evolution lit the fires of modern Christian fundamentalism—argued that anyone who interprets the opening chapters of Genesis literally is foolish.[4] God's truth, he said, is to be found in the spiritual meaning of Genesis. But we'll come back to that a bit later. It's Augustine's treatise *On Christian Doctrine* with which we will presently concern ourselves. It is in this work that Augustine also builds on the work of Origen, his predecessor, and attempts to offer interpretive tools for discerning between the literal and spiritual senses of Scripture.

The key for Augustine lies not in a new interpretive theory but in an old one—one that, even by his day, was already starting to become ancient: the greatest commandment. In Matthew 22—notably just before the so-called Little Apocalypse in which Jesus lays out what judgment day will be like—Jesus has a run-in with his old pals, the Pharisees and the Sadducees. They were up to their old tricks again, trying to expose Jesus as the heretic they thought him to be. The Sadducees tried their hand first, attempting to trip Jesus up with a question about who would be married to whom if, according to the law of Moses, a man died, his brother married the widow, and they all went to heaven. When that didn't work, the Pharisees stepped up to the plate to have a crack at embarrassing Jesus. Instead of trying to trip up Jesus on his interpretation of just one law, they threw the book at him, so to speak, by trying to prove that he didn't understand or perhaps even care about the law of Moses.

One of them, an expert in the law of Moses, asked Jesus, "Teacher, which commandment in the law is the greatest?" (Matthew 22:36). What we see here, in this short question, is an often-overlooked miracle. Calling Jesus "teacher" was likely not a sign of respect, since the Pharisee was there to expose him as a fraud. Rather than admiration, the legal expert's words dripped with sarcasm. That Jesus—God incarnate, who could call down lightning bolts on command—didn't pay him any mind is nothing short of a miracle. What Jesus did say was this: "'You shall love the Lord your God with all your heart, and with all your soul, and with all your mind.' This is the greatest and first commandment. And a second is like it: 'You shall love your neighbor as yourself.' On these two commandments hang all the law and the prophets'" (Matthew 22:37-40).

If you are familiar with this passage, you've probably always focused on the call to love God and neighbor. That's not a bad thing. It's definitely the point Jesus is making and wants us to catch. But we would be remiss if we skipped over that last part—about how all the law and the prophets hang on these two commandments. For the people of God in Jesus' day, the Law and the Prophets were their Scripture, and the very foundation of their faith. So Jesus is saying that if you want to understand what God is trying to teach you through Scripture, that understanding must be grounded in and guided by love for God and neighbor. In other words, the greatest commandment isn't just a call to be nice to people. It's a guiding principle for reading and interpreting the Bible. And that's exactly the point Augustine makes in *On Christian Doctrine* when he writes,

> Whoever, then, thinks that he understands the Holy Scriptures, or any part of them, but puts such an interpretation upon them as does not tend to build up this twofold love of God and our neighbor, does not yet understand them as he ought. If, on the other hand, a man draws a meaning from them that may be used for the building up of love, even though he does not happen upon the precise meaning which the author whom he reads intended to express in that place, his error is not pernicious, and he is wholly clear from the charge of deception.[5]

Augustine is essentially saying that no matter how simple, straightforward, unadulterated, "plain," or rock-solid we think our biblical interpretation is, and no matter how great and meticulous our exegesis might be, if our conclusion doesn't lead us to love God and neighbor as ourselves, then we're wrong. Perhaps more to the point: if we're using the Bible to cause harm to others, we're wrong. Period.

If all Scripture hangs on the greatest commandment, then loving God and loving others should be the standard by which we judge our biblical interpretation. Some may dismiss this as a warm, fuzzy, and relativistic approach to interpreting Scripture. But that perspective would miss the radical implication of Augustine's claim. If Augustine is right, this way of reading Scripture would mean a seismic calamity for much of American Christianity, which is so often driven and defined by condemning others in the name of God. If Augustine is right, then many, if not all, of those "biblical values" we cling to aren't biblical values at all. They're *our* values, cultural and personal values we've simply sanctified with Bible verses. Worse, those so-called biblical values are not just misinterpretations of Scripture; they're blasphemy, because they portray the God of love as a God of hate and oppression.

Our proof-texted biblical values don't leave us morally neutral, the way incorrectly conjugating a Greek verb might do. Those so-called biblical values lead us to do the opposite of what Jesus himself said must be the driving force and guide for our faith, the hook on which everything—*everything*— we believe must be hung. If there are things we believe that don't fit on that hook—that don't lead us to love God and neighbor—then no matter how biblical we think they are, our understanding of the biblical passages we are citing is simply wrong.

Period.

A hermeneutic of love

When we combine Origen's and Augustine's rules for interpreting Scripture, we find an approach to reading the Bible that liberates us from the shackles of literalist fundamentalism and

its offspring, dispensationalism, while restoring the intellectual integrity lost from proof-texting. Most importantly, their
interpretive approach to the Bible refocuses our engagement
with Scripture on the way of Christ. In doing so, the guiding
principles of Augustine and Origen enable us to approach the
Bible not as a weapon with which to beat our opponents over
the head but as a guide for loving God, neighbor, and enemy
alike. It's a hermeneutic of love.

This hermeneutic, or rule for reading and interpreting
Scripture, is summed up well in something else Origen said—a
simple but beautiful statement that captures how and why
the greatest commandment should drive us beyond the literal
words on the page and down deeper to the spiritual truth
of Scripture. Origen wrote that we should try to discover "a
meaning worthy of God in those Scriptures which we believe
to be inspired by [God]."[6] It's such a simple statement on its
face, but given how Scripture is often approached today, it's
a fairly radical claim when you give it some thought. Today,
the Bible is chopped up into chapters and verses, which then
get used to prove our theological agendas and as ammunition
to take down our opponents. We may claim that we are "simply" repeating what the Bible says, but that's never true. What
we are really doing is discovering in the Scriptures a meaning
worthy of supporting our theological preconceptions.

To be sure, Origen came to Scripture with *his* own preconceived ideas and biases, just like anybody else. That's
unavoidable. But Origen had something a lot of us today
are missing: self-awareness. He didn't try to pretend he was
an unbiased messenger for God by simply quoting the Bible
without interpretation. Instead, because he recognized that
his own biases and preconceived ideas would play a role in

his interpretation of the Bible, he sought to combat them by pursuing an interpretation of Scripture that was worthy of his Lord. Since Jesus is God's full revelation, interpreting the Bible to find "a meaning worthy of God" means finding a meaning worthy of everything Jesus taught, preached, and stood for. Finding such a meaning in Scripture will drive us to love God with all our hearts and to love our neighbors as ourselves, just as Jesus commanded us to do.

Of course, we all have preconceived ideas about what Jesus taught, preached, and stood for that come into play too. In our telling of the gospel, Jesus often believes all the things we believe and despises all the people we despise. Which is why we need help keeping our preconceived ideas and biases in check so that as we go about reading the Bible and trying to understand what is being said, we always remain focused on love, just as Jesus was. It is to this end that Augustine steps in to be our guide as we interpret Scripture with his hermeneutic of love. Augustine challenges us to stop and ask ourselves whether the meaning we settle on is worthy of the One who loved so much that he gave up his life to save those who didn't love him back. Or are we so focused on being right and using the Bible as a weapon to attack and destroy our enemies that we don't really care about finding a meaning worthy of the God we claim to follow? Too often the answer is yes.

For centuries the Bible has been used to harm and oppress our neighbors in the name of God. Some 150 years ago, white Christian preachers in the American South had a litany of proof texts to justify slavery. They only cared about the literal words on the page, because diving any deeper into Scripture would have forced them to confront the fact that loving our neighbors means we can't enslave them, even if we have a Bible verse we think lets us do just that. During the Jim Crow era, the Bible was again used to keep races separated, condemn people in mixed-race marriages, and sanctify discrimination against anyone who wasn't white. In more recent years, the Bible has been used in a renewed effort to demonize the LGBT community, cast all Muslims as demonic forces, and ostracize immigrants and refugees. We've always needed a hermeneutic of love for reading the Bible, but as our list of "enemies" seems to grow, perhaps we need it now more than ever.

The great thing about this old, new hermeneutic is that it doesn't require an advanced degree. It certainly doesn't replace traditional biblical scholarship, but most of us don't have PhDs in biblical studies. And yet we still have to wrestle with difficult passages in Scripture. As we do that, a hermeneutic of love challenges us to continually ask ourselves this: Does the meaning I think I've found in a particular passage or verse lead me to love God and my neighbors? By leaning on the teachings of Jesus himself, Augustine and Origen give us a hermeneutic of love that not only teaches us how to read and apply the Bible better but also helps us discover in the mysterious imagery of Revelation a meaning worthy of God.

8

Mill Creek

Some of my best childhood memories were made on Wimpole Drive, the street where I spent several of my most formative years. Our house was in the perfect location. The neighborhood was less than ten minutes from downtown Nashville and the church we attended. The main road running outside our neighborhood was lined with restaurants that everyone from church seemed to eat at on Sunday afternoons after church let out. Best of all for me, my grandparents, who liked to spoil me rotten, lived in the neighborhood right next to ours.

The neighborhood itself was rather quiet. A blue-collar community, its streets were lined with modest, ranch-style brick houses. We lived in one, and my best friend, Chad, and his family lived next door. Behind both our houses ran the peaceful waters of Mill Creek.

Mill Creek was bigger than your typical creek, more like a small river. I can't even begin to count how many hours Chad and I spent exploring its waters and the surrounding woods. We'd fish for what seemed like days, catching mostly small brim, although to us they might as well have been giant marlin. All the bait we needed was right there in the creek, waiting for us in the form of what was then an abundant supply of crayfish. In college I learned it was actually an endangered species called the Nashville crayfish that's indigenous to Mill Creek. I can't help but think we bear no small amount of blame for its endangered species status. I'm really sorry about that one, Planet Earth.

But for as much fun as we had exploring and playing in its peaceful waters, Mill Creek had a darker side. It flooded. A lot. Whenever the forecast called for rain, we made sure to keep a close eye on the creek. And whenever the forecast called for a lot of rain, we made sure to pack a suitcase. Our fears weren't unfounded. When it poured, Mill Creek very quickly turned into a raging torrent. And when it did, my mother always told me the story of two guys she knew in college who tried to kayak the creek while it was at flood stage. They were never seen again. As a kid, I always thought it was nothing more than a boogeyman story meant to scare us into behaving. But it wasn't. One visit to Mill Creek during flood stage should have told me that.

Even though my backyard sat a good ten feet up from the creek, it was little protection. A day or two of rain was enough to raise Mill Creek to the level of our backyard, which was even worse for Chad because his yard sat a foot or two lower than ours. A small drainage ditch that diverted neighborhood runoff into the creek also ran next to his house, which meant their garage and most of his backyard flooded constantly.

When it did flood, it happened in the blink of an eye. That's why we always had to have our bags packed. If the creek rose even a little bit over its banks, our tabletop flat backyards ensured our houses would quickly flood. Yet despite the constant flooding and near misses, my family managed to avoid the worst of it. The same can't be said for Chad's grandparents, who moved into his house when he and his parents moved to Oklahoma, and witnessed devastating destruction to their home during the great Nashville flood of 2010. I was living in Memphis at the time, but I watched it all play out on the news and through constant updates from my family, who still lived in the area, having moved into my grandparents' house in the adjoining neighborhood when my grandmother moved out.

The local meteorologists called it a thousand-year flood. It was unlike anything Nashville had ever seen and probably will ever see again, at least in my lifetime. More than a foot of rain fell in the Nashville area in just forty-eight hours. The Cumberland River that runs through downtown Nashville burst its banks and flooded several blocks of downtown, including a storage facility used by several Nashville musicians, who saw their guitars and equipment, for some their entire livelihood, destroyed.

Further upriver, the Cumberland flooded a popular mall and the luxury Gaylord Opryland Resort and Convention Center that stands next door. Water rose at least two feet high in the mall, and rumors spread that the aquariums in the aptly named Aquarium Restaurant had burst and that sharks were swimming the corridors where shoppers once roamed. Water got high enough in the hotel that its occupants had to be evacuated and ended up spending the night in the gym of a nearby high school.

Mill Creek, of course, flooded too. Worse than it ever had before. I'll never forget the picture of Interstate 24 where it crosses Mill Creek just outside downtown Nashville. The water was so high all you could see were the tops of cars that had been trapped in the rising water. A portable classroom from a local school had been lifted off its foundations and was floating down the interstate.

The flooding on Wimpole Drive was just as catastrophic. My parents, along with several of our friends and family, rushed over to help Chad's grandparents evacuate from their house. They worked to save as much as they could, but there was little they could do. Chad's grandparents made it out okay, but the creek that usually just soaked the backyard and floor of the garage nearly covered their entire house that day. The floodwaters rose all the way up to the roof. Remember how I told you how we packed our bags whenever there was the threat of heavy rain in case we had to flee quickly? That wasn't hyperbole. The water rose so fast that day that my mom's car was completely flooded even though it was parked on the other side of Wimpole Drive, a good distance away from the creek. She and several others who were helping Chad's grandparents evacuate had parked there thinking their cars would be safe because the creek had never come anywhere close to rising that high before. But it did that day.

More than two dozen lives were lost as the result of the flood. Countless homes and businesses were destroyed. The city of Nashville eventually dried out, but the memory of those days are seared into the town's collective memory for generations to come.

Chaotic waters

Flood stories tragically play themselves out around the world every year, as they have throughout human history. From the yearly monsoon rains in India to the annual flooding of the

Mississippi, from the devastation of Hurricane Katrina to the mythical global flood of Noah's day, the devastating force of water has played a powerful role in the lives and imaginations of people of all places, times, and beliefs.

This was certainly true for people living along the Mediterranean Sea in the first century, and for the apostle John when he was exiled on an island there when he had his famous revelation. The people living along the shores of the Mediterranean Sea two thousand years ago knew just how deceptive and dangerous its sparkling blue waters could be. The countless wrecks that now litter its seabed are an eternal testament to how easily the waters of the Mediterranean Sea can turn dark and stormy, destroying lives and livelihoods.

The same was true of the Black Sea, the great body of water not too far north of Patmos, where some scholars think the story of Noah might have originated. Whether the story of Noah has its roots there or not, similar stories of destruction could be told about any major body of water anywhere in the ancient world. From the Jordan to the Nile and everywhere in between, storms, floodwaters, and even pirates were a constant threat to life on the rivers or open sea.

It should come as no surprise, then, that water became a powerful image in ancient literature, including the Bible and the book of Revelation. The sea, in particular, became an iconic image of power, destruction, and chaos throughout the entire Old and New Testaments. The story of creation begins with God hovering over the dark chaotic waters at the dawn of time. Just a few chapters later, the world is covered in a catastrophic global flood. As the children of Israel flee Egypt, they find themselves trapped between Pharaoh's army on one side and a foreboding sea on the other. Forty years later, another body of water, the Jordan River, stands between them and the Promised Land. In Job, the power of God is displayed in God's control over the raging seas and the terrifying monsters that dwell in their waters. Jonah is famously cast overboard in the midst of a storm, in hopes of calming the chaotic waters. In the Gospels, Jesus and his terrified disciples find themselves adrift in stormy seas. And while on one of his many mission trips, Paul encountered a storm that left him shipwrecked.

Water gives life. But in the ancient world, water in the form of oceans and seas, rivers and lakes was also a symbol of chaos and destruction. It's no accident, then, to see that image appear over and over again in the pages of the Bible. But it's not there to simply reinforce the fear of stormy seas and raging rivers. The people of God already knew that fear well. The biblical writers also used water to confront that fear with hope.

The disciples were terrified, alone in a storm on the Sea of Galilee, until Jesus walked across the water, conquering the chaos and calming the storm. Jonah was cast overboard into the tempest only to be rescued by God in the most unlikely of ways. Job stood awestruck at the mighty power of God, but found peace in God's healing grace. The Jordan River raged before the children of Israel until God intervened to let them cross into the Promised Land on dry ground. Before Joshua parted the river, Moses parted the sea, giving Israel not only a way to escape but a path to their future. The floodwaters of Noah's day covered the entire earth, but God protected Noah and his family from death and destruction. The waters at the dawn of creation were dark and chaotic, but God ordered the chaos and brought from it life and everything we see around us.

And at the end of all things, when there is a new heaven and a new earth because the former order has passed away and there is no more sea (Revelation 21:1), it's not the beach we're losing. It's the pain and destruction, the loss and heartbreak that come from the chaotic waters. Chaotic water is an apocalyptic metaphor that John's original audience would have easily understood. If we can understand that simple image too, we can begin to unlock the mystery of Revelation and rediscover the apocalyptic roots of the Christian faith.

Deciphering the meaning of images like "no more sea" in Revelation is not an easy task. Revelation's symbolism is so radically foreign to us today that it really shouldn't come as a surprise to see some folks look at that imagery as a hidden code to be deciphered. But to approach it as a hidden code to be deciphered is to read Revelation as a literal text. To stay at the literal level of the text—to say, for example, that Revelation 21 claims that God is going to get rid of the ocean—is to completely miss the deeper spiritual truth that John is trying to reveal. That truth is wrapped up in apocalyptic imagery, symbolic language that functioned both to protect John from the power structures and authorities he was criticizing and to open up Revelation and allow it to become a text that can speak to the church throughout the ages, regardless of time or place. To accomplish both these tasks at the same time, John utilized the transcendent power of myth.

Myth, history, and truth

Myth has become something of a dirty word in the church, particularly in fundamentalist and dispensationalist circles that insist on reading every page of Scripture literally. But myth plays an important role throughout the Bible, and especially in Revelation. The problem we have today is that we have been conditioned to think of myth and history in contrasting terms.

We've been taught to believe that in order for something to be true, it must be literal history. We say that myth, therefore, is not true because it did not take place literally in history. As a result, myth has become a synonym for "not true." Dispensationalism, then, with its roots in fundamentalism, can't embrace myth, because it is convinced that for something to be true, it must literally take place in history.

You can see this conundrum in the evolution versus creation debate. While a literal six-day creationism has become de facto orthodoxy throughout much of American Christianity, the insistence on a literal reading of Genesis is a fairly new phenomenon. The insistence that Genesis had to be read literally arose in direct response to the perceived threats of Darwinism, which in the minds of many of Darwin's day and many more still today, juxtaposed Genesis to science because in order for Genesis to be true it had to be literally and historically true. There was no space for the truth found in myth.

You can certainly find literal readings of Genesis throughout the history of the church, but that's not how it has always been read or how the Jewish tradition that wrote the story of creation demands it be read. In fact, the Jewish tradition that gave birth to Genesis has long read the creation account as myth. Likewise, as we saw before, the great church father Saint Augustine said way back in the fourth century that anyone who reads the creation account in Genesis literally is foolish for doing so. And yet both Augustine and the Jewish tradition regard Genesis as true. How can that be? The answer lies in liberating ourselves from the need for something to be literally or historically true in order for it to convey or contain truth. Myths can be true, whether or not they literally happened. Take the tale—or myth—of Chicken Little. Talking chickens don't exist, but the truth of the story—that constant paranoia and overreaction can destroy your credibility, and that loss can have serious consequences—is true nonetheless.

Not everything in the Bible is myth, of course. The Bible is made up of all sorts of genres of literature—from poetry to history to gospel to apocalyptic. But the Bible also takes advantage of the power of myth. Why? Because myths can convey transcendent truths that can be shaped and contextualized over time to better fit a particular context and yet still contain the same basic truth. Myths have a power to convey truth that literal events don't always have. That's what we see in the book of Genesis, both in the creation account and later on in the story of Noah. Both myths are borrowed from older stories in other cultures and have been shaped and contextualized to meet the needs of the biblical writers. Nevertheless, they are true, and true in the truest sense of the word. They are true in the sense of the message they convey: that God is at work in the world, creating and caring for God's people.

Revelation is a book of myth. Dragons and plagues and multiheaded beasts populate the book. That doesn't make it any less true, nor does it mean the things it speaks about won't happen. It is, and they will. But it's the truth *behind* those events that Revelation is trying to convey, not their literal happening in history.

The myths of Revelation also play another important role: they subvert the myths of those in power, in this case, Rome. Much like the early church appropriated "Caesar is Lord" by saying instead "Jesus is Lord" in order to convey the truth, Revelation takes myths, sayings, and images known to its original audience and subverts them with new myths, sayings, and images. In doing so, Revelation sets up an alternative way of living, an alternative truth to that which was proclaimed by the empire.

Whereas the empire conquered through violence and power, Revelation tells of a slaughtered lamb who conquers with the power of his word (Revelation 5). Whereas Rome told the myth of an all-powerful, perfect empire, Revelation tells the story of a beast rising out of the sea who is utterly flawed and destined for destruction (Revelation 13). Whereas the empire tells the myth of the Pax Romana, Revelation tells of peace for all, not just the elite, who always find a way for others to fight their battles for them (Revelation 21–22).

Myth allows Revelation to tell the truth in proactive ways that capture the imagination. The drama in Revelation helps readers to not only remember the events of the book but also remain open to more than one dogmatic interpretation. The text of Revelation is alive, and is ever open to new interpretations in new contexts and historical settings. Such is the power of myth. It's a power that apocalyptic literature like Revelation takes full advantage of, not just for the sake of dramatic storytelling or even to convey the truth but to serve as a call to action.

The unveiling

While Revelation may come at the end of the New Testament, apocalyptic theology was central to Christianity from the very beginning. The focus of Jesus' ministry was the dawning of the kingdom of God and the unveiling, or revealing, of the truth about what that kingdom looked like. As I mentioned earlier, that is, after all, what *apocalypse* means: "an unveiling." This is exactly what John is doing in his apocalypse: he's unveiling the truth of the state of the world both now and in the soon-to-come future.

Jesus' ministry was also apocalyptic, although his unveiling of the truth was directed toward the religious institutions of his day rather than the church, as it did not yet exist. But it is that calling to account, and Christ's overall call for repentance, that has many scholars viewing Jesus as an apocalyptic prophet. He didn't tell stories of dragons and talking scrolls like John did. Rather, he is seen by those scholars as an apocalyptic prophet because he believed the last days were at hand. He went around warning people about the end, preparing them for judgment day by calling on his followers to repent and promising justice for the oppressed.

The letters of the apostle Paul also reveal an apocalyptic worldview.[1] His letters disclose a man convinced that Jesus was about to return any day and a theology thoroughly shaped by that conviction. One example of that conviction is his view of marriage. Paul didn't seem to think marriage was all that important, and even advised people to stay single if they could (1 Corinthians 7:1-7). Paul wrote this not because he was opposed to the institution of marriage but because he wanted Christians to focus the entirety of their time and attention on preparing for what he thought was the imminent return of Jesus.

But once again, apocalypse doesn't necessarily refer to the end of the world. Through modern movies, books, comics, and, ironically, even the church, we've become conditioned to equate apocalypse with the end. But again, translated literally, *apocalypse* simply means "an unveiling." That's the key point of Revelation. For all its talk about the end, its focus is on the unveiling of truth to the people of God. This truth had just as much to do with their present as it did with their future. In that sense, John isn't just writing apocalyptic literature. He's also following in the rich tradition of the Old Testament prophets.

Now, you're probably thinking to yourself, "Of *course* Revelation is Bible prophecy! It's, like, *the* prophetic book of the Bible." The thing is, it is and it isn't. Revelation is definitely in the prophetic tradition of Scripture—just not in the way you're probably thinking or folks like Jack Van Impe would have you believe.

Prophesying about the present

Unlike the colloquial use of the word *prophecy* today, biblical prophecy has very little to do with predicting the future. Prophets like Isaiah and Jeremiah did warn about the future, but not like Nostradamus. They were, on behalf of God, issuing warnings about what would happen if the people of God didn't repent from their wicked ways and restore justice to the land. The prophets weren't fortune-tellers. They were warning the people of God about what would happen in the future if they did or didn't act a certain way in the present. Which is why biblical prophecy is about the present as much as or more than it is about the future.

This is exactly the dynamic we see in Revelation. John begins his apocalypse with a word from Jesus to seven then-present-day churches (Revelation 1–3). He's not telling their fortune; he's giving them instructions for how to live in the here and now. How they do that directly affects what is to come in the future. But the focus of John's prophetic words from Jesus are on the present, just as they would be from any Old Testament prophet.

In fact, John explicitly declared himself to be a prophet in the final chapter of Revelation (see Revelation 22:9). Several times throughout his apocalypse, he draws from the language and imagery of the Old Testament prophets. The words of

Isaiah are referenced repeatedly, most directly in Revelation 21, which draws from Isaiah 65:17: "See, I will create new heavens and a new earth. The former things will not be remembered, nor will they come to mind" (NIV). A command for John to eat the scroll is likely drawn directly from Ezekiel 2:8-10. There are echoes of Hosea marrying the prostitute Gomer in John's invocation of a prostitute to describe the people's idolatry (Revelation 17–18). And there are also echoes of Amos's poignant cry to "let justice roll down like waters, and righteousness like an ever-flowing stream" (Amos 5:24) when John describes the song of the 144,000 sealed servants of God as being like "the roar of rushing water" (Revelation 14:2 NIV).

Revelation also comes back, time and time again, to the contrast between true and false prophets. The warning against false prophets comes up repeatedly in the letters to the churches before becoming a key part of the apocalyptic imagery later on, when the false prophet of the beast appears. The reason for this concern about false prophets is because John's task in writing Revelation was to reveal, or unveil, the truth. After all, that's what an apocalypse is all about. False prophets lead people astray from the truth, but real prophets like John proclaim the truth about God. That truth is a call to repentance and justice lest the people of God suffer judgment.

So rather than being biblical versions of Nostradamus, the prophets were more like your mom when you were a teenager, warning you to get off your phone before you lose privileges to it forever. You may end up losing your phone, but it wasn't because your mom was psychic. It was because she warned you what was going to happen if you didn't listen, and because she had the power to ensure those consequences came to pass,

they did. The same thing was true for Israel and the prophets—except that God, being God, could ensure that those consequences would come to pass no matter how smooth a talker
you thought you were or how sneaky you thought you could
be by stealing your phone back while your mom was sleeping.
In other words, biblical prophecy isn't about predicting a set-
in-stone future. It's about what will happen in the future if the
words of the prophet are not heeded in the present. Nothing
here is about the fortune-telling power of the prophet; everything is about the power of God.

The key to Revelation's place in the tradition of biblical
prophecy, then, is not in its ability to predict future events but
in its often-overlooked call to repentance, and its promises of
liberation and justice. Revelation is, if it is nothing else, a sustained critique of Rome, for which the ancient enemy of Israel,
Babylon, plays the role of stand-in. Rome is Babylon, the great
oppressor, not just of the people of God, but of anyone in the
ancient world who stood in its way.

But Israel had another ancient oppressor: Egypt. For John's
first audience, the parallels between Revelation and Exodus
also would have been striking, as both tell the tale of liberation
from oppression by way of plagues that afflict the afflicters in
order to set the afflicted free. But plagues aren't the only invocation of Exodus in Revelation. In fact, the entire section on
the seven trumpets and bowls of wrath can be seen as reimagining the story of Exodus when God besieged Egypt with
plagues until the people of Israel were liberated.[2] Exodus is
also invoked in the opening chapter of Revelation, when God
is described as "who is and who was and who is to come,"
an echo of God's name as revealed to Moses: "I am who I
am" (Revelation 1:4; Exodus 3:14). The prayers of the people

of God for deliverance in Revelation are just like the cries of the people of God in Exodus 2 and 3, as is the reference to "mourning and crying and pain" (Revelation 21:4), which likewise conjures up the cries of Israel in Egyptian bondage.

Retelling the story of God's faithfulness, and reminding people that they follow the God of Abraham, Isaac, and Jacob, the God who brought them out of Egypt, are recurring themes throughout the Old Testament in both the Prophets and elsewhere. But as an apocalyptic prophet, John goes even further. John doesn't simply retell the story of the Exodus for the church; he takes on the mantle of Moses and attacks the system of oppression under which they were living. Calling out injustice was a key task of any Old Testament prophet, who didn't just warn the people to repent of their sins but also offered hope in the form of a promise that God was already at work, breaking into their present to create a new future.

Justice revealed

Nearly every apocalyptic image John uses in reference to Babylon (that is, Rome) is a direct attack on the imperial system of oppression and injustice of his day. The beast comes from Babylon not as a special, set-apart figure but as the embodiment of a system and empire that is fundamentally antithetical to the way of Christ. The way of Jesus is love of enemies, peace, plenty, and life eternal. The way of Rome, or Babylon, is "conquest, war, famine, and death."[3]

In the kingdom of Jesus, everyone shares what they have and none go without, for all are equal (Acts 2:42-47). In the kingdom of Caesar, as John describes particularly with the third horse of the apocalypse, economic injustice reigns and the chasm between rich and poor is not only immense; it is

unbridgeable. Likewise, when John describes the great whore
of Babylon, he's attacking not prostitution or women but the
economic injustice of the Roman Empire, which got rich by
preying on the weak and vulnerable throughout the empire.[4]

Like the story of Exodus, Revelation promises that justice
and liberation are coming, that those Rome has oppressed
and exploited will soon be liberated, healed, and welcomed
into the promised kingdom of God. It's that promise of justice
that should further reshape our understanding of Revelation,
moving it away from book of apocalyptic terror and toward
a message of hope. Being able to see that promise of hope
for justice in Revelation is a challenge for most of us. If this
is the first time you've thought about the book of Revelation
in terms of things like economic and social justice, you're not
alone. That was certainly the case for me, even long after I
gave up my addiction to *Jack Van Impe Presents*. Back when I
thought Revelation was a road map to the future, if someone
had tried to tell me that it was actually a prophetic call to
justice, I would have assumed they were on drugs or, worse,
were a godless liberal.

As my old, rapture-loving self would have done, you may
even consider such a reading to be *eisegesis*: that is, a reading
of a text that projects one's own presuppositions and biases
onto it in order to find a meaning one wants to be there but
isn't actually supported by the text itself. If that's the case,
trust me; I get it. It's hard to think about biblical prophecy,
Revelation, and the apocalypse as anything other than gloom
and doom about the future. But the reason we struggle to see
such a prophetic call to justice isn't the obscurity of the text
itself, the graphic imagery, or even the dispensationalist conditioning many of us were raised with, although those things

surely play a role. The reason most of us struggle to see Revelation as a prophetic call to justice is because we are blinded by our own privilege.

It's hard to see the cry for liberation and justice when we have no need for liberation and justice in our own lives. That's not to say that because we're not dirt poor or from a developing country that we haven't been wronged in life, haven't had to struggle, and aren't in need of some sort of justice. But if you're anything like me and you grew up as a straight, white, middle-class conservative Christian in the United States, the idea that Revelation is about liberation, justice, and transformation in the here and now and not a secret road map to your mansion in heaven? Well, it can sound as bizarre as a ten-headed beast or a guy eating a scroll.

The royal life

The theologian Walter Brueggemann would call this life of privilege "the royal tradition."[5] Not because any of us are royalty, but because relative to our neighbors in other parts of the world or even just across town, our lives are more akin to the biblical kings than to their subjects, in whose shoes we typically place ourselves when we read the Bible. Brueggemann argues that when we read the Bible it actually takes less imagination than we might assume to see ourselves in the life of an Old Testament king like Saul or David even though, on the surface, their lives may seem radically foreign to our own.[6] But if we live in North America, chances are our lives have a lot more in common with royalty like Saul and David than we realize. For example, where our next meal will come from, or if it will come at all, is not something most of us give much thought to. In the context of the world of the Old Testament, that fact puts us far closer to the life of Saul or David than to the lives of their subjects. The same is true for access to things like medicine and education. The degree of medical care and education we take for granted would have been reserved for royalty in Saul and David's day.

We don't have to search too hard to see how this sort of privilege of the royal tradition exhibits itself in our lives today. Countless Americans are inoculated against seeing the suffering of our neighbors and having basic empathy for them, not to mention the urge to serve. Take, for example, the Black Lives Matter movement. It arose out of a long, painful history of black men, women, and children being killed both at the hands of police officers and extrajudicial mobs, who were often white and often have not been held accountable in any meaningful way. Protests, including marches through the streets and sit-ins on the highway, have been held across the country. Those unaffected by the tragedies, including white people of varying degrees of socioeconomic standing, often dismiss the cries of the Black Lives Matter protesters as nothing more than complaining. Little credence is given to what the protesters are saying, because the lives of those dismissing their cries are so far removed from the life experience of the protesters, are so privileged in comparison, that the separation is almost as stark as that of King Saul and the people of Israel. Even the word *protest* seems almost dismissive of what is happening because they're not simply expressing disapproval; they're fighting for their lives.

Or consider the Trump administration's decision to separate immigrant children from their parents at the U.S.-Mexico border. Although the decision was met with horror and outrage across the United States and around the world, the response

among the 81 percent of white evangelicals who voted for Donald Trump was noticeably different.[7] Some have tepidly criti-
cized the practice, conceding that there was probably a better
way. But a life of ease has kept them from empathizing with the
plight of the families involved, and endless opportunities in the
States keep them from seeing that the reason so many entered
the country improperly was not out of a disregard for law and
order, but out of desperation and a willingness to do whatever
they had to do to rescue themselves, or at least their children,
from violence, oppression, and hopelessness.

Sadly, these are but two prominent examples of what is too
often a daily way of life, a life of taken-for-granted, oblivious
privilege that allows too many people—mostly white, American Christians like me—to go about thinking our lives are
normative and that anyone who deviates from our sense of
normalcy must be doing so for malicious and sinful reasons.
This is why Revelation is so hard for so many of us to understand, particularly as a prophetic call to justice. As New Testament scholar Barbara Rossing explains, "Victims of injustice
have a special window into these stories that affluent Christians cannot fathom. Like the plagues of Exodus, the stories
of Revelation speak most clearly to people who struggle under
oppression—to 'God's little people,' as South African Allan
Boesak calls them. For the rich and comfortable, the plagues
sound vengeful and terrifying. But to people suffering under
oppressions the plagues are good news because they herald the
end of the oppression itself."[8]

The Latin American theologian Pablo Richard goes
even further:

Cosmic agonies of this kind, however, are not "natural"
disasters but rather the direct consequences of the structure

of domination and oppression: the poor die in floods because they are pushed out of safe places and forced to live alongside rivers; in earthquakes and hurricanes the poor lose their flimsy houses because they are poor and cannot build better ones; plagues, such as cholera and tuberculosis, fall primarily on the poor because they are malnourished. . . . Hence the plagues of the trumpets and bowls in Revelation refer not to "natural" disasters, but to the agonies of history that the empire itself causes and suffers; they are agonies of the beast caused by its very idolatry and lawlessness. Today the plagues of Revelation are rather the disastrous results of ecological destruction, the arms race, irrational consumerism, the idolatrous logic of the market, and the irrational use of technology and of natural resources.[9]

In other words, dispensationalists have one thing right. The book of Revelation is perhaps more relevant today than it ever has been—just not for the reasons they suggest.

Relevant Revelation

Revelation is relevant today but not because of events unfolding in Israel. Revelation is relevant today because the plagues it warns about are all around us. There are no winged beasts flying through the skies, or horsemen riding on pale horses, but the plagues they bring with them—famine, poverty, economic injustice, ecological disaster, death—are all very real today.

The reason some of us look for those beasts in the pages of the Left Behind series, rather than recognizing them in Revelation for what they are, is that they're not a reality for most of us. Privileged people like me turn to the fictionalized version of struggle and pain because we can't relate to the epic struggle to survive and the pain of oppression that gave birth to Revelation. Most of us don't worry about where our next meal will come from, or whether our home will disappear because of rising ocean levels. The four horsemen who bring death and destruction (Revelation 6:1-8) are an apocalyptic fantasy for most of us living in places like the United States. For countless people around the world, they are a daily reality.

That's what makes Revelation so hard for many of us to understand, yet so powerful for those to whom it speaks so clearly. You and I can still find hope and comfort in the idea of a new heaven and new earth—absolutely. But just imagine the overwhelming sense of joy that comes with the promise of peace from chaotic waters when you have had to watch your child drown in the sea as you fled a war zone. Imagine the joy that would come with rescue if rising sea levels meant the coastal village in which your family had lived for generations was about to be underwater. Imagine struggling with hunger for a lifetime but now getting to eat endlessly from the tree of life for all eternity. Or consider those unable to pay for a doctor, who have witnessed a never-ending stream of loved ones lost to disease and death—how they would rejoice at the promise that death and mourning and sorrow will soon be no more.

The reason I first turned to Jack Van Impe and folks like him is the same reason anybody first turns to people like that: Revelation is hard to understand, and these self-proclaimed experts promise to make it all clear and easy. And in their own, woefully incorrect way, that's exactly what they do. They take mysterious images and give them not only a clear meaning but also a clear purpose. They make a foggy future clearer. Actual biblical scholars, of course, can do a far more accurate job of clarifying mysteries of Revelation. But the fundamental reason most of us struggle to understand Revelation isn't our lack of fluency in biblical Greek or our lack of knowledge of specific apocalyptic imagery and tropes. The reason most of us struggle to understand Revelation is because it wasn't written to us or with us in mind. And I don't just mean readers in the twenty-first century. I mean any of us throughout history who were or are too privileged, too safe, or too comfortable to understand what John is trying to say. John is writing to real churches with real people who were suffering real injustice and persecution. And I don't mean the kind of persecution that includes not hearing the cashier at Target tell you Merry Christmas.

John's apocalypse is both a call for justice and a promise of liberation. On both counts, it is hard to fully appreciate or understand when we ourselves have little real need of justice or liberation. John could leave out the images of dragons and beasts and scrolls and replace them with bland, unimaginative, straightforward language, and it still wouldn't fully resonate with most of us. He is simply speaking to a need we simply don't have, or else don't think we have.

So while books like the Left Behind series and the accompanying movies play up the fear and terror that can be mined from the pages of Revelation, that fear and terror is fundamentally misplaced. John did not write the book of Revelation to strike fear and terror into his readers. He wrote it to inspire hope. If anyone should be terrified of what John has to say, it is those in places of power and privilege who use their power to oppress the weak.

Revelation promises that the fears of the oppressed will soon cease as their oppressors finally face the justice of God. Those who have spent their entire lives living on the underside of history will finally move from fear to hope when the Lord returns.

But that hope isn't a passive promise, an excuse to sit by idly waiting for God to act.

It's a call to action.

The present *kairos*

The task of any biblical prophet, including John, is not simply to reassure readers that everything will be taken care of in the future, but to call them to action and repentance in the present. That way they will be ready for that future day, because it is coming soon. That future does ultimately depend on God. But, as Jesus taught us to pray in the Lord's Prayer, we have a role in bringing that future about in the present by living out God's will and incarnating God's kingdom on earth as it is in heaven.

The terrifying imagery of Revelation itself plays a role in that work. Like any prophetic warning, it's intended, as my grandmother would say, to shake some sense into folks—in this case, the authorities it was criticizing and the people it was calling to repentance. Jesus was on his way back, and he was coming with swift justice. The message of Revelation isn't that all hope is lost, but rather "There's still time, but repent before it's too late!" This is true both for the powers that be and for the laity, as we see in the open letters to the various churches, particularly Laodicea, who is warned to shape up lest Jesus vomit them out of his mouth (Revelation 3:16).

But this effort to call the people to repentance and conversion isn't about simply getting them to say "I'm sorry." Nor is it exhausted by the sort of intellectual assent to a list of ideas or beliefs that we often associate with repentance and conversion today. The sort of repentance and conversion that John the Revelator and the rest of the biblical prophets are concerned with is a call to justice, a call to love the least of these and to welcome and care for the marginalized and oppressed. It's a call echoed in Isaiah 1, when God tries to rattle the people of God into repentance by telling them he's disgusted by their offerings and will listen to their prayers no more—or at least not until they wash themselves clean by seeking justice, rescuing the oppressed, defending the orphaned, and pleading the case of the widow (Isaiah 1:16-17).

The biblical prophets weren't just trying to shake sense into people. They were trying to teach people how to live the way God intended. That's why, along with apocalypse and prophecy, Revelation also falls into another biblical category. This genre is often overlooked, but when it is understood, it helps to unveil not just the full meaning of Revelation but its call for the people of God. You see, while the book of Revelation is filled with all sorts of apocalyptic imagery, that imagery is wrapped up in the form of a letter. In the beginning of Revelation, we see seven real letters to seven real churches. John's apocalypse begins the same way you would begin any letter: with a salutation. John greets the seven churches, giving them his regards before conveying the message, or revelation, that Jesus has given to him for each of them. John also ends his apocalypse like a letter, with a personal closing that gives further instructions.

Why does it matter that Revelation is written as a letter? Because it sets the framework for understanding the entire book of Revelation. Aside from being an apocalypse, Revelation also functions like an epistle. Epistles, like Paul's letters to other churches of the time, gave practical advice for how churches should function and how their people were to live their lives as followers of Jesus. That's exactly what John is doing at both the beginning and end of Revelation. He's telling people in the seven congregations how to live in the end times. Just like Paul, John was convinced that the return of Jesus was imminent, and he shaped his guidance for the church with that in mind.

Revelation's identity as an epistle can completely transform how we read and understand its apocalyptic imagery. Like the letters that frame the book, the Apocalypse of John is a story for the people of God now, not in some distant future. John is preparing the church for what is about to happen. He is calling them to repentance and transformation now, not later, because the apocalypse is already starting to unfold. John's audience is already living in the last days because Jesus had been raised from the dead, ushering in the dawn of all things being made new.

The central focus of Revelation is the resurrection of Jesus, and like Paul, John understood the resurrection as more than a onetime event. It was this sense of ultimate deliverance that drove Paul's apocalyptic imagination. In his theology, the resurrection of Jesus was only the beginning. For both John and Paul, Jesus was the "first fruits" of a new creation (1 Corinthians 15:20-23). His resurrection was but the beginning of resurrection for everyone. In keeping with their Jewish roots, Paul and John understood resurrection to be something that happened to everyone at the same time, much like the valley of dry bones the prophet Ezekiel watched come back to life individually, but all together (Ezekiel 37). Therefore, if Jesus had been raised from the dead, it had to mean the resurrection of everyone else and the end of the present age were right around the corner.[10] Resurrection as John and Paul understood it was a communal, not individual, experience.

So, if Jesus' resurrection is the beginning of the end times, then Revelation isn't dealing with events in the distant future, though those events are there at the end of the book. Revelation is preparing the church for the present. John calls this present time a *kairos*, or an opportunity for grace and conversion, because, for all the graphic apocalyptic imagery, Revelation is calling the church to repentance so that through the redemptive grace of God, the church can avoid the punishment of the beast and his followers.

It's this present kairos that Jesus is talking about when he addresses the seven churches at the beginning of Revelation. He isn't telling them to wait to get things squared away. He's calling them to repent and transform now because he is coming soon. In fact, he is already standing at the door knocking, waiting for them to let him in to complete the work of resurrection and re-creation. Ironically, that image undermines our idea of the second coming as the return of Jesus to be with his people. But it makes perfect sense when we think back to Jesus' promise to his disciples at the end of Matthew's gospel. Jesus promised his disciples that he would be with them always, even to the end of the age (Matthew 28:20). The cry of the church in Revelation isn't as much a cry for Jesus to come back in the future as it is for Jesus to act in the present.

As we've seen, modern anticipation of the rapture has dispensationalists feeling free to ignore pressing problems like creation care and poverty, because Jesus will be back any day to make it all better. But for John, Paul, and the early church, imminent judgment didn't mean abandonment of discipleship. Rather, it meant doubling down in earnest, because final judgment was at hand. They recognized that the time for repentance was almost gone, because the end of the age was at hand. The end of the age, not of the world or of history. Even in its promise of a new heaven and a new earth, Revelation is not describing the end of this world. Rather, as Paul puts it, the form of this world is passing away and being renewed, re-created (1 Corinthians 7:31).

This is why Martin Luther is said to have declared that if he knew the world were to end tomorrow, he would still plant a tree. He knew how invested God is in the here and now, and he knew that, as a Christian, he was called to that same sort of investment. Luther recognized that the promise of a new heaven and a new earth doesn't absolve us from caring for the present one. Why? Because God's promise is one of renewal, not starting over from scratch. As Paul said, it is the form of the world that is passing, not the world itself. We have a responsibility, a calling, to help usher in that new form now as it is promised in Revelation.

In Revelation, heaven is not so much a destination as it is a source of hope and inspiration. The New Jerusalem isn't a goal as much as it is a way of life that is about to dawn on earth. It's effectively an answer to the prayer Jesus taught his disciples to pray, "Thy kingdom come, thy will be done, on earth as it is in heaven." In Revelation, Jerusalem is portrayed as a city "coming down" to earth. It is the job of the church to prepare the way of the coming kingdom: the new heaven here on the new earth. This is why Revelation shouldn't be understood as an invitation to passivity. Revelation isn't an excuse to sit around and wait for God to act. It's a call to action and a guide for how to live in the last days, in preparation for the dawning of the New Jerusalem.

Revelation isn't a road map to the future. It's a model for how to live in the present. The transcendent utopia of its final chapters isn't just a far-off promise. It's something akin to the Lord's Prayer. John isn't just revealing what will happen one day. He—or more accurately, Jesus—is calling the people of God to live out that kingdom now on earth as in heaven. This is why it is so important that we not miss the role Revelation plays as a guide for life in the present, not just the future. This is, after all, why John's apocalypse begins with letters to churches in the present, with instructions on how to live in the here and now. The apocalyptic life isn't defined by sitting around and patiently waiting for God to act. It's defined by living out the promised kingdom of God on earth as it is in the final chapters of Revelation.

This is what makes the book of Revelation not just an apocalypse but also gospel. It is truly good news to the poor, good news for the oppressed, good news for the hungry, good news for the lost, the least, and the dying. It promises that the dead will live, the broken will be healed, the first made last, the hungry fed, the oppressed liberated, and the poor crowned as royalty in a new kingdom. To understand the apocalyptic gospel better, we need to put down the dispensational charts and predictions, get out of our theological bubbles, and start serving and listening to those people we would otherwise ignore—the kind of people to whom John wrote his reve-lation. They weren't the elite, the wealthy, or the privileged. They were the outcast, the marginalized, and the oppressed. They were outsiders in an empire where their faith made them a target for persecution. Their way of life ensured hardship, ridicule, and even the prospect of martyrdom. And yet they loved their neighbors and enemies in the empire anyway.

The key to understanding Revelation isn't hidden in a secret code. It's found in love for our neighbors. It's found in loving the neighbors we forget even exist or, worse, blame for their struggles. It's found in listening to the cries of Black Lives Matters activists instead of dismissing them as thugs and hooligans. It's found in listening to the survival stories of immigrants instead of portraying them as rapists, murderers, gang members, and dangerous criminals. It's in opening our doors to refugees in desperate need of saving instead of turning them away because we're worried they might be terrorists.

It's in imagining new and creative ways to bring justice to the poor and liberation to the oppressed that we will find a meaning in Revelation that's worthy of God. The true wonder of Revelation is found not in the apocalyptic imagery but in its proclamation that God is already at work in the world. God is already healing, liberating, and reconciling everything in creation back to our Creator. And God invites us to do these things with him so that one day all these things will be made new on earth as it is in heaven.

9

Saved

Not long after my internship in the swamps of Florida, I moved to the Mississippi Delta to take a job as the director of student ministries at a Methodist church in Memphis, Tennessee. The church had a long-standing relationship with the United Methodist Church in Nicaragua. Well before I arrived, the Memphis congregation had been taking teams of adults to Nicaragua to build churches while sending money and other donations in the intervening time to help out however they could.

My second year in Memphis, our church's Nicaragua team leader and I decided to make the annual Nicaragua trip a youth trip. I went to Nicaragua with him the summer before we planned on taking the teens. That way I could scope things out myself and get the lay of the land. Then together we spent the next year preparing and training our senior high students for the trip to Nicaragua. In many ways, it was your typical overseas short-term youth mission trip, though without the typical construction projects. We primarily led vacation Bible school programs for the children, feeding them and fellowshipping together over lunch each day. It was during lunch one of those days that something happened that forever changed my understanding not just of missions but of the gospel itself.

The lunch we served each day was typically the same—emphasis on *served*. We didn't make the food. The women in the local church made it, which is why it smelled delicious and not—had we attempted to cook it—like a steaming pile of mystery garbage. The routine was the same every day. The women cooked the food while we sang songs, played games, and taught Bible lessons to the children. Once lunch was ready, all the children lined up to eat. It was always a bit chaotic at first, but the lunch line formed quickly, almost spontaneously. The kids knew the routine well, as we were hardly the first short-term mission team to come their way.

The food, usually some combination of rice and chicken or some other meat, was often served in a bag. This may sound odd to you, but it's fairly typical of Nicaragua. If you drive up and down the streets of any major city in the country and come to a stop at a red light, someone will likely approach your window with a dozen or so bags filled with various fruit juices hanging from a pole. It looks weird to outsiders like you and me, and obviously people in Nicaragua do use cups, but bags are a cheap and efficient way to store and drink juice on the go. The same is true with food. While you're more likely to find juice being sold in bags, those same bags worked just as well for lunch. And at a vacation Bible school, bags not only make for easy prep; they cut down on some of the mess that usually comes with kids and plates filled with food.

One day we were hosting vacation Bible school at a half-finished church outside the small mountain town of Estelí. (*Half-finished* might be a bit generous; it was a concrete foundation surrounded by cinderblock walls whose exposed steel skeleton reached unimpeded to the heavens, as the church still lacked a roof.)

The church itself was nestled in the heart of a small neighborhood. The houses in the neighborhood were roughly constructed wooden shacks, made from hand-hewn planks and topped with corrugated steel. The modest homes were lined sporadically across a handful of dirt roads. Some had electricity running to them, but many did not. All had dirt floors that were conspicuously well maintained by the women of the neighborhood, who could regularly be seen sweeping the floors of their homes, stopping only to smile and wave as we walked by. They may not have had much in that little mountainside neighborhood, but they took great pride in what they did have, and it showed.

When the announcement was made to line up for lunch, the kids in our half-built church dropped whatever they were doing and ran to get into line. At the same time, countless other children we didn't even know were there emerged from the shadows of nearby houses and joined the frenzy. There was only space in the church's makeshift kitchen for a couple of students to help serve at a time. So those of us who weren't serving lunch either waited in line, chatting with the kids, or sat down to talk with them while they ate their lunch. Or at least tried to talk. Most of us didn't speak much Spanish and most of them didn't speak English, but the kids politely smiled and justifiably laughed as we tried to patch together our limited Spanish vocabulary into a fully formed sentence. Which rarely, if ever, happened.

The lunch line was chugging along when a youth worker and I noticed that every once in a while, a kid would grab a bag of food and, instead of finding a place to sit on the church floor, would dart outside and run away as fast as their little legs could carry them. Being oblivious American short-term missionaries, we were a little miffed. I mean, we had come all this way from Tennessee to hang out with them. Heck, we had even footed the bill for their lunch, and they didn't even have the decency to say thank you, let alone stay and talk? The nerve! How were we going to save their souls if they wouldn't hang around long enough to learn how sinful they were?

So after the fourth or fifth kid had darted out of the church, we decided to follow them, assuming they were probably gathering just around the corner with their co-conspirators, reveling in their mischief of having pulled one over on the dumb gringos.

We waited by the door of the church until our moment came. It didn't take long before a small boy, maybe seven or eight years old, went running outside, blowing by us so fast we could barely keep up. Thankfully, for my pathetically out-of-shape self, he didn't go far. We followed him down the road, around the corner, and down a small dirt path, thinking we were just moments away from stumbling upon the group of lunchtime hooligans we knew had to be lurking somewhere close by.

Then all of a sudden, he disappeared inside one of the small wooden houses.

From a distance, we couldn't see exactly what was going on, but we could see what looked like another pair of hands reaching out from the darkness to take the bag of food.

"Aha! We've finally found them!" I thought to myself.

But as we got closer to the house, a bit of light began to break through the space between the corrugated steel roof and the wooden planks precariously holding it aloft. There wasn't a lot of light, but there was enough to illuminate what was really going on.

There was indeed another set of hands reaching out to grab the bag of food, but they weren't the hands of his co-conspirators.

They were the weathered hands of his mother. He was bringing his lunch home to share with her and his baby sister. It was likely the only meal they would have that day.

We stood frozen in our tracks, slack-jawed and dumb-founded. As we tried to regain our bearings, we looked around and realized this lunchtime ritual was playing itself out all throughout town. It was why all those kids grabbed their bags of food and ran away so quickly. And it broke me completely.

Even as I write this now, nearly a decade later, the tears flow as freely as they did that hot and humid afternoon in the Nicaraguan countryside. Tears of heartbreak that any family anywhere would live that close to the brink of starvation. And tears of humiliation and shame as it finally dawned on me just how privileged I really am, how ignorant I am of the struggles and hardships the rest of the world faces, and just how fundamentally I don't understand the gospel.

I was there to save Nicaraguan souls, but what they really needed was their daily bread.

Salvation now

Before that moment, salvation, or "getting saved," had always been something I thought of in strictly spiritual terms.

Salvation affected my life in the here and now only insofar as it ensured I didn't do this or that so that I could go to heaven after I died. Growing up, my family was far from well off, but I was a white, middle-class kid who never worried about where my next meal would come from, never thought twice about being able to afford a doctor's visit, and never set foot on a dirt floor. The only thing I needed saving from was hell. The gospel was good news to me only because of what it did for me in eternity.

I was a pastor and lifelong Christian when I went to Nicaragua, but I was still clueless about the gospel. I was clueless about why Jesus called the gospel good news for the poor (Luke 4:18). I was clueless that "Thy kingdom come, thy will be done, on earth as it is in heaven" was anything more than a fancy way of saying "Bring on the second coming!" I had no real need for the kingdom to come in my life. I had my daily bread. My life was comfortable, safe, privileged. The only thing I thought I needed saving from was an eternity in hell.

I had long ago asked Jesus into my heart, but he had stayed there. Transformation, to me, was about making a person sinless, entirely sanctified, perfect. It never occurred to me that transformation might be something that happens here and now in ways other than not drinking, swearing, or having premarital sex.

I didn't understand the real promise of the end times, because I didn't understand the sort of salvation it was promising. I didn't understand that the salvation it promises isn't waiting till the end of time; it's breaking into the here and now, on earth as it is in heaven. My faith had been so self-centered and so spiritualized that aside from imparting a great deal of guilt and shame, it had no real effect on my life in the present.

For all my self-professed expertise on the gospel and the end times, it turned out I knew very little about either. This boy and his family and his entire neighborhood understood what made the promises of Jesus good news far better than I did or ever could. They were the ones who had been blessed and told that theirs is the kingdom of God. They were the ones who understood the hope that came with Jesus' promise that the first would be made last. They were the ones who could truly appreciate the coming of a new world where pain and sorrow are no more, where every tear is wiped away and the tree of life is open to all so that none go hungry ever again. They understood that salvation and the hope of Revelation are good news because of what they promise in the here and now, not just after we die.

I knew nothing. For me, Christianity was a religion of ideas and the end times a puzzle to figure out. I was so fixated on avoiding hell and not being left behind that I never stopped to consider anyone's needs but my own. My faith had been unraptured long before I went to Nicaragua. But when I watched that little boy give up his lunch to feed his family—people I had come to "save"—the rest of my faith began to unravel too. I realized just how little I really understood about salvation, and how clueless I was about what made the gospel truly good news.

I had left the rapture behind, but I hadn't abandoned the rapture mentality. Christianity, for me, was still all about getting to heaven. The myopic focus of end-times theology is but the by-product of the American Christianity that has fostered it for so long—a Christianity focused on the future like a zero-sum game, a faith so overspiritualized and focused on heaven that it has no practical relevance for the here and now. So even though I had abandoned the rapture, I never really gave up the mentality from which it sprang.

That's why folks like the families in that small mountain town in Nicaragua understand the book of Revelation far better than I ever did or will. It was written to people like them: people in need of hope and salvation, not from eternity in hell, but the hell of this life—the hell of poverty, oppression, and injustice. People who know what hunger is and can actually appreciate the miracle of being able to eat freely from the tree of life. People who by accident of birth don't have the "right" nationality, "right" skin color, "right" socioeconomic standing, or "right" language and are effectively barred from participating in the economic and social systems that gave me comfort and privilege. It's almost as if they hadn't even been given a chance to take the mark of the beast so they could buy and sell and have a shot at a comfortable life. I, on the other hand, bore the mark obliviously. Born by chance into the privilege of the empire, I never stopped to consider that so many of the opportunities I take for granted every day are out of reach for countless people simply because of who they are, where they're from, and what they look like.

I always thought gold streets and pearly gates sounded neat, like icing on the cake of my well-deserved heavenly mansion. I couldn't even begin to imagine the hope those iconic images inspired in people whose floors were literally made of dirt and whose walls were built from whatever scraps of wood they could scavenge together. When Jesus said he came to proclaim good news to the poor, set the prisoner free, heal the sick, and rescue the oppressed, I thought he was being poetic. That family in Nicaragua heard a gospel whose good news didn't wait for them on the other side of death, but affected their lives now to transform and save them from the hells of poverty, oppression, racism, and injustice.

It had been nearly a decade since I lost my faith in the rapture, but Nicaragua taught me that I still had plenty of my end-times faith left to be unraptured. Being raptured hadn't been my goal in a long time, but I still saw getting to heaven as the whole point of being a Christian. Christianity was still all about me and my eternal reward. After that day in Nicaragua, I had to face the fact that I hadn't just been wrong about the rapture. I had been wrong about Christianity, wrong about the gospel, wrong about salvation, wrong about what it means to be a follower of Jesus. Christianity wasn't all about me and my reward. It couldn't be that self-centered and that self-serving. If it was, it wouldn't be worthy of bearing the name of Christ.

So if the rapture was no longer my hope, and heaven alone wasn't the goal of salvation, then what was left?

What was the point of being saved?

What was the point of being a Christian at all?

Red-letter Christianity

To my surprise, the answers to my post-rapture questions of faith came not from a theology book, but from an old man with a spitting problem.

That man was Tony Campolo. Campolo is a professor emeritus at Eastern University and a prolific speaker, writer, and former spiritual advisor to President Bill Clinton. When I first heard him speak at the National Youth Workers Convention, I was familiar enough with his reputation to know not to sit too close. Campolo is notorious for spitting when he talks. Not on purpose, obviously, but the guy is a one-man Bellagio fountain when he talks. That night a group of smart-aleck youth workers staked out front row seats for Campolo's talk and arrived dressed in yellow ponchos to protect them from the imminent saliva storm. Campolo got a good kick out of it.

The theme of Campolo's talk that night was the same theme he's preached on for years: red-letter Christianity. It's the same theme that led him and Shane Claiborne to create an organization called Red Letter Christians. As the name implies, it's a conviction that the words of Jesus that are often represented in red letters in our Bibles should drive our understanding of the gospel and, with it, the Christian life. In other words, our understanding of Christianity should fundamentally be a red-letter theology.

"But what about Paul and the rest of the New Testament?" you ask. Or at least I did that night, in the form of a snarky text message to Campolo I started to type out when he opened the floor to digital questions. The short answer is, Campolo and Claiborne love the apostle Paul. They love the rest of the Bible too. They're not dismissing Paul or any other part of Scripture. What they're trying to do is live like Christ as authentically as they can. To do that, they make the actual words and teachings of Jesus, the red letters, the lens through which they understand not just the rest of the Bible, but the faith itself.

But I was too busy that night trying to formulate my snarky text message to hear that explanation. I was just about to hit "send" on my phone when Campolo began telling a story that made me forget all about trying to anonymously debate him and had me considering the possibility that maybe they were onto something with their whole "let's take the words and actions of Jesus seriously" pitch.

The story Campolo told that night was of a meeting he once had with a student and the student's father. I've since heard other people tell a similar story, so perhaps it was more anecdote than autobiography. Or maybe it's just a common occurrence when people come face-to-face with something Jesus said that they don't like. Either way, as he told the story, the student's dad was angry with Campolo for teaching all that red-letter nonsense in class. Or more accurately, he was angry that his son was taking it too seriously—especially the stuff about nonviolence and giving what you have to the poor. The father had demanded a meeting with Campolo to find out exactly what he was teaching his son and whether it really was as "extreme" as what his son was telling him.

So Campolo calmly explained red-letter theology to the father, and the father not-so-calmly let him know what he thought. "I'm a Christian too," he said, "and I'm fine with all of that stuff in the red letters. But only up to a point!"

"And what point is that?" his son interjected. "The cross?"

It was as if that kid had reached out of the story and punched me right in the stomach.

Here I was, texting away with my theologically superior insight, when I suddenly came face-to-face with two realizations: one, I was far more passionate about talking about faith than living it out; and two, as much as I'd like to be the student with the zinger, the reality is I was much more like his dad, following Jesus . . . up to a point. For me, that point was turning my faith into real, Christlike action. I mean, feeding the homeless at Christmas or going on a short-term mission trip or faking a famine for thirty hours with my youth group? I was there. But real, lasting Christlike action in the way I lived and moved and had my being in the world each and every day? Not so much.

Naturally, I was mad at Campolo for his surprise checkmate right when I was trying to checkmate *him* with my text message. But I was also intrigued. So when I got back to my office at church the next week, I decided to do a little digging and find out what else this crazy, spitting preacher had to say.

Judgment day

My search led me to YouTube, that great bastion of randomly uploaded videos. It wasn't quite as vast back then as it is today, but it was still wide enough in scope to house a few Tony Campolo videos. I found several clips of him going more in depth about what it means to be a red-letter Christian. And then I found the one video that I still can't stop quoting to this day.

It was an interview Campolo gave to a Canadian television show called *The Hour.* The show opened, as most talk shows do, with the host introducing Campolo. The two of them chitchatted about Campolo's time as spiritual advisor to the president before they started talking about Red Letter Christians. And that's when Campolo began to rebuild my shattered understanding of the gospel and salvation.

> The only description that Jesus gives of judgment day is how we treated the poor. On that day, he's not going to ask you theological questions. He's going to ask—you know, it's not going to be "Virgin birth? Strongly agree? Agree? Disagree? Strongly disagree?" You know . . . it's going to be, here's what it's going to be—the twenty-fifth chapter of Matthew: "I was hungry. Did you feed me? I was naked. Did you clothe me? I was sick. Did you care for me? I was an alien. Did you take me in? What you failed to do to the least of these you failed to do unto me, because I'm not up in the sky somewhere, I'm waiting to be loved in people who hurt, and as you relate to people who hurt, you're

relating to me." There is no Christianity that does not tie us
up with the poor and the oppressed of the world.[1]

Here, at long last, staring me right in the face, was the key
to surviving judgment day. I had spent so many years trying
to find it, trying to figure out how to make sure my name was
written in the book of life. I had searched high and low, turned
to every expert I could find, but the answer wasn't written in
black-and-white propositions of theological dogma. It was in
the red letters of Jesus. The answer was here, in the words of
Christ, who could actually tell me with real authority what
would happen on judgment day.

According to Jesus himself, when judgment day finally rolls
around, he won't be standing at the pearly gates, asking us
what we believe; he'll be asking us what we did. Specifically,
he'll ask how we cared for the least of these. My theology
should inspire me to care for the least of these. If it doesn't,
then I can have all the right theological answers but still not
love my neighbor. In that event, I will find myself shouting
back to Jesus like a resounding gong or a clanging cymbal:
"Lord, when did I see you hungry or thirsty or a stranger or
needing clothes or sick or in prison, and did not help you?"

This was a radically different version of both salvation and
faith than I was accustomed to. As I had understood it, Jesus
died to save *me* and to keep *me* from going to hell. My job was
to "accept" that gift by not sinning too much so I could go to
heaven. But here, in the Little Apocalypse of Matthew 25, I
saw a version of Christianity defined by earthly concerns. It
was a form of salvation focused not on me and what I believed
but on others and how they were cared for.

If what Jesus said in Matthew 25 is true, then Christianity
isn't defined by the sort of individual, personal relationship

with Jesus that I had always been told was what makes Christianity so great. If the red letters of Matthew's apocalypse are true, then Christianity is about a communal relationship with Jesus and the ones he came to serve and save. Christianity is personal; it's just not private. It's personal in the sense that it drives us towards loving, personal relationships with others. Salvation isn't about "Jesus and me." It's about *us* and all of creation. Which makes sense if you think about it: to be Christian is to be Christlike, and Christ came not for himself but to give his life for others because God so loved *the world*.

If the apocalyptic vision of Matthew 25 is true, then serving others isn't a secondary response to our salvation; it's *how we are saved*. Not in the sense of how I get to heaven, but in the true biblical sense of salvation. Salvation isn't an individual reward but a creation-wide act of God's grace into which we've been invited to participate by incarnating God's love to the lost, the least, and the dying. If following Jesus means being Christlike, and if Christ came to incarnate the love and grace of God to a broken world, it only makes sense that salvation wouldn't be a moment of instantaneous personal reward. Salvation is an invitation to die with Christ to our self-centeredness in order to devote our lives to others and their needs just as he did. In this way we are all together transformed through the power of the Holy Spirit into the new creation promised in Revelation and realized in the resurrection.

Faith or faithfulness?

If you grew up a red-blooded American Protestant Christian like me, then this probably sounds like the dreaded works-based salvation we were taught to despise. We were told that Christianity was all about a personal relationship with Jesus, that all you had to do to be saved was believe, say the Sinner's Prayer, confess your belief in Jesus, and you would go to heaven. But that understanding of salvation is a fairly recent development in the history of the Christian faith. How Christians understand salvation has evolved over time. How people think we are saved today hasn't always been how people throughout history have thought we are saved.

Jesus himself changed the salvation paradigm from the sacrificial system that came before him. But that wasn't the last time the people of God's understanding of salvation changed. In fact, salvation in the Judeo-Christian tradition doesn't actually start with the sacrificial system. After all, many people came before the sacrificial system was institutionalized in the law of Moses: people like Joseph, Sarah, and Abraham. The Christian faith considers them all to be "saved," so to speak, but not because they made the correct atoning sacrifices. So how were they saved? The writer of Hebrews tells us it was their faithfulness to God's calling, not their adherence to a list of rules or set of beliefs that didn't yet exist, that "saved" them (see Hebrews 11). This emphasis on actions rather than ideas is important to keep in mind as we begin to rethink salvation in light of the apocalypse, because it reveals what biblical faith is all about. Biblical faith is not defined by rules, rituals, or ideas; it's about faithfulness to a calling from God.

Of course, the law of Moses did eventually arrive, and with it a new path to salvation—or more accurately, atonement. The law of Moses laid out in detail what would keep the people of God in right standing with God. Some 613 commandments in the Torah told them what they would need to do or not do and what sacrifices they would need to make to get back in right standing—atone for their sins—when they screwed up.

Curiously, heaven doesn't really come into play here or really anywhere throughout the Old Testament. The people of Israel certainly believed in the existence of heaven, but going there wasn't the goal. In fact, the Old Testament includes only a few mentions of people going to heaven, and they were taken there directly by God while they were still alive. Faithfulness for the sake of faithfulness, and the better life now that came from that faithfulness, was the "goal." Going to some otherworldly paradise or avoiding eternal conscious torment? These simply don't appear in the Old Testament.

When Jesus shows up on the scene, the history of salvation takes another dramatic turn. When he was crucified, the veil in the temple, symbolically separating the people from their God, was torn apart. Access to God was now open to all. The sacrifices once required for atonement are no longer required, according to the apostle Paul, because Jesus was the final atoning sacrifice. Through his sacrifice we are all forgiven and brought back into right relationship with God. Yet Paul describes *how* we are saved in a fascinating way. Salvation is, Paul writes, "not by the works of the law, but by faith in Jesus Christ" (Galatians 2:16). In this passage, Paul uses the Greek term *pistis Christou*, which has often been translated "faith in Jesus Christ." Some biblical scholars suggest, however, that a better rendering of Paul's words would be "faith *of* Jesus" rather than "faith *in* Jesus."[2] Better still would be to translate *pistis Christou* as "faithfulness of Jesus." At first glance, this may seem like an insignificant detail, the kind of thing scholars like to dissect. But the implications for our understanding of salvation are enormous. It's not our belief in right ideas that saves us, but rather Jesus' faithfulness in following the will of his Father, even to the point of the cross. It's the same sort of faithfulness the patriarchs exhibited before the law of Moses was even given.

For Paul, faithfulness doesn't stop at the cross. As he says in Philippians, we are called to that same faithfulness, called to have the same mind in us that was in Christ Jesus that "though he was in the form of God, did not regard equality with God as something to be exploited, but emptied himself, taking the form of a slave, being born in human likeness. And being found in human form, he humbled himself and became obedient to the point of death—even death on a cross" (Philippians 2:6-8). For Paul, having the same mind as Christ doesn't mean believing the exact same ideas as everyone in the pew next to us. It means pursuing the same way of life, the same sort of faithfulness to God's calling that Jesus embodied.

James builds on this understanding of faithfulness—answering God's calling to a particular way of life—in his own epistle, in which he famously says that faith alone does not save us, for faith without works is dead (see James 2:14-26). When many of us hear the word *works* today in the context of salvation, we've been conditioned to think about actions intended to win God's approval through moral perfection. But when James talks about works, he's not talking about the sort of rituals, or *works*, of the law of Moses that were intended to make atonement with God and which Paul said Jesus replaced the need for when he writes in Romans that "a person is justified by faith apart from works prescribed by the law" (Romans 3:28). There's another kind of *works* mentioned in the New Testament, and it's the kind that James is talking about here. The *works* James describes are better understood in English as *faithfulness*, the kind of faithfulness that Jesus and the patriarchs embodied. Faithfulness is a work of faith defined not by adherence to religious rituals or by intellectual assent to a list of beliefs, but by a particular way of life that is faithful to God's calling—especially God's call to love God with all our heart, mind, and soul, and our neighbor as ourselves (Matthew 22:36-40). By being faithful to this calling to love our neighbor, we're not trying to win God's approval or love. We already have God's love, by virtue of God's loving nature. We love our neighbors not as a means to our own end of getting to heaven but as an end itself. To love them simply for the sake of trying to win God's approval would be to objectify our neighbors by turning them into a means to an end. If we did that, we would still be doing the sort of ritualistic "works" of the law that Paul says won't justify us with God anyway.

Unfortunately, this sort of nuanced balance between belief and putting that belief into practice was lost over time, and the church found itself back in a place where religious rituals, or "works," were once again taught to be required for salvation. Selling indulgences is one example. This is the sort of thing Martin Luther railed against and why he was so emphatic about salvation by faith alone. That zealousness was not without problems, though, for Luther decried James as a "gospel of straw" and wanted it cut out of the Bible for its emphasis on works. The legacy of Luther's distaste for James has turned the book's testimony about the critical importance of works into an awkward part of the New Testament for Protestants rather than an important reminder to live out our beliefs.

Luther's legacy, Protestantism, centered on the doctrine of salvation by faith alone, an idea that continues to be not only embraced but celebrated by countless Christians today. But the history of salvation didn't end with Luther. If anything, Luther's ideas laid the foundation for yet another development in the history of salvation. Centuries later, as the Western world found itself in the throes of the Industrial Revolution, salvation by faith alone came to its logical, literal conclusion. The revivalism of nineteenth-century America transformed salvation once more. The Industrial Revolution transformed the way we think about life, particularly in regards to time. Journeys that once took weeks on horseback could now be completed in days on a train. Manufactured goods that once required several days to make by hand could be created in a single afternoon thanks to the advent of the assembly line. But industrialization didn't just transform transportation and manufacturing. It transformed society as well. It transformed us into an on-demand people who expected to get places quickly and have what we want immediately. The church was not immune from this transformation. The church's approach to salvation soon began to mirror the same sort of assembly line logic, demand for immediacy, and focus on the bottom line of the Industrial Revolution. By taking salvation by faith alone at its literal word—that is to say all that is required for salvation is belief—salvation became an industrial process as the way of Jesus was streamlined and ultimately replaced with an easy-to-follow and incredibly efficient system guaranteed to produce salvation every time.

Folks like the evangelist Charles Finney created salvation factories, of sorts, with their own assembly lines. Meeting at first in the theaters of New York City and then spreading out to revivals in towns across the country, Finney would bring a sinner up to the stage, where the sinner would sit in a chair, known as the mourner's bench, and confess his or her sins. Confession made, salvation was had, and it was on to the next sinner, who would come on stage and take a seat in the chair.

Replace the stage with a sanctuary, and the chair with an altar to kneel at, and you have a typical Sunday morning at any evangelical church in America today.

In the holiness tradition in which I was raised, Phoebe Palmer took things a step further and declared that "the altar sanctifies the gift," meaning a visit to the altar was enough to be instantly and entirely cleansed of sin, or as Nazarenes like me call it, entirely sanctified. Palmer and Finney were far from the only ones promoting a streamlined version of salvation focused on the bottom line of getting to heaven. Countless other evangelists and preachers contributed to this sort of reductionist version of salvation. Regardless of where we trace its origins, the result of the various incarnations of American Christianity was that salvation by faith alone became Christianity by right belief alone. Christianity was individualized, internalized, and spiritualized. Discipleship was replaced by a moment of decision. The way of Jesus was replaced with the Sinner's Prayer. Salvation became a zero-sum game in which all that mattered was avoiding hell, and doing that became as simple as saying a few magic words at an altar. A particular way of life no longer really mattered, because it was no longer ultimately necessary for salvation. Sure, we'll say we need to act like Christians and we're quick to condemn people for not conforming to whatever our particular version of cultural Christianity dictates—like no smoking, drinking, or getting tattoos. But the rest of our life belies the truth that faith excuses a multitude of sins.

This is how 81 percent of white American evangelical voters can support someone like Donald Trump whose words, actions, and policies are so radically antithetical to the way of Jesus. The disconnect between faith and faithfulness means self-professed Christians can support all sorts of unchristian things without feeling hypocritical because their Christian faith (and personal salvation) is ultimately determined by what they believe, not by how they live. None of the doing of Christianity matters when the only concern is getting to heaven.

Dispensationalism grows in the fertile soil of a faith whose focus is on the afterlife and having all the right answers. The "ends justify the means" ethics of end-times theology is a natural outgrowth of an individualized, internalized, and spiritualized version of salvation. So end-times theology isn't the disease that needs to be eradicated in order for Christianity to rediscover what it truly means to follow Jesus. It's just a symptom of a much deeper problem—namely, the disconnect between the Christian *faith* and the Christian *life*. For in its pursuit of escape from the earth, end-times theology reveals a problem that runs throughout Protestantism in general and American Christianity in particular: a self-centered Christianity exhausted by simply agreeing that a certain list of doctrines are true.

The irony is that, properly understood, end-times theology can rescue the church from an individualized and over-spiritualized understanding of salvation. For what we see in John's apocalypse is the apocalyptic truth of Matthew 25 unveiled. Now, Revelation does not directly quote Matthew 25, as it does some of the Old Testament prophets, but the call of Matthew 25, and the consequences for not heeding that call, shape the first several chapters of Revelation. There are echoes of Matthew 25 at the end of John's apocalypse as well, when Jesus declares, "My reward is with me, and I will give to each person according to what they have done" (Revelation 22:12 NIV).

The first chapters of Revelation don't get as much attention as the rest of Revelation, at least not in dispensational circles. But if we take another look at the letters contained within them and let those letters become the framework for understanding the rest of Revelation, as John intended them to be, the curtain begins to be pulled back on the message of Revelation in general and salvation in particular. They emphasize the importance of "works" when it comes to the last judgment while also setting the time frame for the message of Revelation as the present, rather than the distant future. Everything that John warns is to come is directly connected to and dependent upon what happens "now."

In six of the seven letters found in the opening chapters of Revelation, Jesus, speaking through John, says, "I know your works," and in the letter to Thyatira he specifically says, "I will give to each of you as your works deserve" (Revelation 2:23). It's a theme that's repeated throughout the book of Revelation: the idea that punishment and rewards would be doled out not on the basis of affirmation of faith but according to how faithful the early church was to God's calling not just to preach but to live out the good news of the gospel. In other words, as anathema as it might sound to Protestant ears, according to Revelation, salvation is fundamentally connected to what we do in this life, not just what we believe.

This didn't create as much tension for John's original audience as it does for Protestant audiences today. For one, "works"-based salvation had a strong foundation in Jewish theology, as we can see in both the sacrificial system and the various rites and rituals that were required of the people of Israel. Paul certainly emphasized the role of faith in salvation, but the role of works in living out that faith wouldn't be as contradictory as we've been conditioned to believe. The work Paul rejected as necessary for salvation was not the working out of our faith by loving and serving our neighbor, but rather the "works prescribed by the law."[3] It's this subtle but important distinction that is the key to resolving any tension between works and faith as they pertain to salvation. When we talk about "works" pejoratively, we usually mean the kinds of rites and rituals required by the law of Moses, the law that Paul says we are no longer under because of God's grace. But as Jesus lays out in Matthew 25, work or effort is very much involved in salvation, just a different kind of work: the work of loving and serving the least of these.

The tension, then, between Paul's teaching on faith alone and James's declaration that faith without works is dead, can be resolved if we substitute the word *love* for *works*. After all, love is what all the works required by the law and the prophets hang on, according to Jesus (Matthew 22:40). Incarnated love is what the prophets called the people of God to embody; the incarnated love of God in the form of Jesus is what saves us; and the absence or presence of incarnated love is what the churches of Revelation are either chastised or praised for. Or to put it another way, it's the love of the Father that creates us, the love of the Son that saves us, and the love of the Spirit that compels us to love one another. This doesn't negate the role of faith, because biblical faith doesn't reside only in the mind; it is lived out in the form of faithfulness or acts of faith—specifically, acts of love. In that way, "faith alone" *does* still save us. This approach also explains why Paul's teaching that faith is the mechanism of salvation became a matter of such heated debate in the early church. It wasn't just that he was ministering to Gentiles and welcoming them into the people of God because of what they believed. The uproar Paul encountered in his ministry came about because he was redefining what was required to be or live as the people of God. He wasn't dismissing the role of works so much as redefining them—just as Jesus did with the greatest commandment and his description of the last judgment.

It's this reimagining that John echoes in Revelation. Works are critical in the book of Revelation, not just because they are how our eternal fate is determined in the last judgment, but because these new works usher in or have ushered in or should have ushered in (depending on which church is being addressed) a new way of life. This is why Jesus continually says, "I know your works" to the seven churches. The people in these communities of faith have been called to live a particular way in the last days, and are not to simply sit around and wait for Jesus to return and make everything better.

The reason most of us reject works when we talk about salvation is not just because of a few verses in Paul's epistle, but because we've been taught that salvation requires perfection, and because we could never be perfect in our actions. No matter how many good works we do, we need Jesus' perfection to save us. But salvation in the Bible was never about moral perfection. It couldn't be. Only God is perfect. Salvation in the Bible is always about right relationship between us and God lived out through right relationship with our neighbors.

Which is why the sort of works-based salvation that Revelation teaches and Jesus describes in his Little Apocalypse of Matthew 25 describe our relationships with others, not how perfect we are. The same is true throughout the New Testament whenever the subject of works comes up as they relate to salvation. The works that James and Jesus and John and even Paul had in mind weren't about moral perfection; they were about love. We don't have to be perfect to love one another. Rather, it's that love that perfects us. As we love one another as God first loved us, we fulfill Jesus' command to "be perfect as your heavenly Father is perfect" (Matthew 5:48) because the heavenly Father is perfect love.

This is why when Revelation talks about salvation and works there is never a demand for perfection, just effort. Moral perfection is never even hinted at in John's apocalypse. And in the epistle of James, which is so famously adamant about the role of works, perfection isn't something we achieve; it's a gift from God. Trying to love our neighbors is what matters, not doing it perfectly all the time. Being Christlike doesn't mean being perfect. It means incarnating love as Jesus incarnated love for us, rather than keeping that love to ourselves. Revelation, James, and the Little Apocalypse of Matthew 25 are so emphatic about "works" because salvation is something God is doing in and through us—not just to save our souls but to redeem and restore the entire world. "Works" are critical in how Revelation, James, and Jesus teach salvation not because the work of loving and serving the least of these is what saves us. Rather, the work of loving and serving the least of these is what we've been saved to do.

Maybe we *have* been left behind

Many of us have been taught to understand salvation as the finish line of our faith and heaven as the reward for crossing over. But salvation isn't a finish line. It's just the beginning of our journey of faith. Jesus doesn't tell his followers, "Okay, now you're saved; go in peace." He says, "Come and follow me." Salvation is an invitation to participate in something much bigger and greater than ourselves. That's what we see in the Gospels, and it's also what we see in Revelation. Revelation is bringing to fruition the call Jesus left his disciples with when he went before them to prepare for the coming of the kingdom of God (see John 14:1-4). But Jesus didn't leave them behind to sit around and wait for his return. Jesus told his disciples, "Go and do likewise" (Luke 10:37). They were to go and do as he had done, and Jesus promised to send his Holy Spirit to guide and empower them as they carried out the work of the gospel. Salvation was never meant to be an escape plan. Salvation is an invitation. We are saved to serve neighbor and enemy alike so that through that act of love, through incarnating God's love to the world, we help bring heaven to earth.

So end-times theology does get one thing right. We *have* been left behind—just not in the way we have been led to believe.

We haven't been left behind by Jesus as a punishment. We've been left behind with a calling: to bring the good news to the poor in every corner of creation, to care for the least of these wherever and whoever they may be, and to lay the groundwork for the kingdom of God coming down to earth as it is in heaven. This is why, when the disciples asked Jesus to teach them how to pray, Jesus taught them how to live. That is, after all, what prayer is really all about: formation. When we pray, it's not just idle talk or pleading. Prayer reminds us of what is important and what needs to be done. Prayer compels us to become God's agents of grace in the world.

At the heart of the Lord's Prayer is a cry and a calling that completely upends rapture theology: "Your kingdom come, your will be done, on earth as it is in heaven" (Matthew 6:10 NIV). The prayer functions as an extension, a reminder, of Jesus' message. Jesus brought the kingdom of God with him, and it is the disciples' job to spread that kingdom to the very ends of the earth after his resurrection.

Rapture theology does the opposite of the Lord's Prayer. It's not focused on bringing the kingdom of God to earth, because its primary concern is escaping the earth. If the earth will be destroyed and Jesus will do all the work of making things new, why bother worrying about it now? The Left Behind books make this rejection of the Lord's Prayer in a subtle but power-ful way: every member of the Tribulation Force carries a gun, but not once in the entire series do they ever say the Lord's Prayer.[4] The Lord's Prayer is key to understanding both the gospel of Jesus and life in the last days because it's a prayer of salvation both for the one saying the prayer and for the entire world. Revelation isn't an afterword to the Bible. It's the answer to the Lord's Prayer. When the old order of things passes away and there is no more sorrow or mourning or hun-ger or death, and when the powerful have been made low, and when the last have become first—then God's kingdom will have come down to earth as it is in heaven.

But praying for that day to come is not an idle calling. It is, like salvation itself, an invitation to participate in the pro-cess by living out what we pray. As a vision of the promise of God's redemptive love fulfilled, Revelation serves as a guide for the present to help us live the kind of life that begins to bring that heavenly kingdom to earth. The firstfruits of that work began when Jesus walked out of the tomb on Easter morning. After his ascension, we were left behind to see that work through until his return, when Jesus will bring that work to completion. But as John and Paul saw, Jesus' resurrection means our work and the promise of Revelation aren't two separate events. Jesus' resurrection means that the work of ushering in a new heaven and a new earth has already begun.

We really *are* living in the last days, as my professor tried to explain to me years ago—the days when God is at work in the world, healing and redeeming all creation. The last days don't start after a fictional rapture, when God finally shows up so the process of reconciliation can begin and end at the same time. The last days started when Jesus was resurrected. They end when he returns.

As much as this sort of approach to the last days differs from end-times theology, it isn't a radically new idea. It's as old as the Christian faith itself, because it comes directly from the New Testament. By centering the Matthew 25 call to apocalyptic love, people like Tony Campolo aren't doing something new. They're just preaching the gospel.

Fundamentally, apocalyptic love is what the gospel is all about. This kind of incarnated love reveals the good news and resurrecting power of Jesus at work in the present, because it makes loving people rather than ideas the center of the Christian life.

At the heart of the gospel is the incarnation of divine apocalyptic love. The incarnation proclaims the good news that God didn't stay disconnected and disinterested, far away in heaven. God put on flesh and dwelled among us, became one of us to know us better. Through that incarnated grace, God redeems all creation. Rapture theology is the opposite of incarnation. It's all about escape. It's about getting away from here and over to there. It's about leaving behind the earth and everyone in it for heaven.

The incarnation is about bringing heaven to earth. It's about God coming down to where the trials and tribulations are, not leaving God's people behind to suffer alone. That's where salvation is found: in the reconciling of all things back to their Creator, in the making new of all things, in love putting on flesh. It's a process that began with the resurrection of Jesus and which we are invited to participate in by taking up our own crosses, dying to self, and following him.

This is why salvation requires work—not the kinds of rituals and sacrifices spelled out in the law, but the harder work of loving our neighbors and enemies alike. This is also why salvation is based on love alone: the love of God that saves us, and our love for God, which responds to that first act of love by loving our neighbor. That kind of love takes work. Not perfect work, just work. It's about doing the work of Matthew 25, work as it's understood in the greatest commandment—the kind of works James said are required to keep faith alive. It's the work of love, of incarnating the love of Christ to the least of these wherever they are, whomever they are, and in whatever way they may need the love of Christ.

Apocalyptic love isn't a warm fuzzy kind of love that makes us feel good about ourselves or affectionate toward others. Nor is it the kind of love that stays hidden in our hearts like faith stuck in our heads. It's the kind of love that boy in Nicaragua showed to his family, the kind of love his entire community needs us to show to them—love in the form of bread and shelter, clothing and medicine. It's the transcendent love of God made present in the here and now. It's the kind of love that reveals the truth of Revelation, because in those acts of love, the former things begin to pass away, as through us God continues to make all things new.

It's the kind of love the prophet Martin Luther King Jr. pro-claimed in the final sermon he gave before he was struck down by an assassin's bullet.

> It's all right to talk about long white robes over yonder, in all its symbolism. But ultimately people want some suits and dresses and shoes to wear down here. It's all right to talk about streets flowing with milk and honey, but God has commanded us to be concerned about the slums down here and his children who can't eat three square meals a day. It's all right to talk about the new Jerusalem, but one day, God's preacher must talk about the new New York, the new Atlanta, the new Philadelphia, the new Los Ange-les, the new Memphis, Tennessee. This is what we have to do.[5]

10

The Last Days

It had been a long time since I watched an episode of *Jack Van Impe Presents*. But as I finished writing this book, I decided to pay Jack and Rexella a virtual visit to see what they were up to these days. What I found was sad. A quick Google search led me to the online home of Jack Van Impe Ministries. Featured prominently at the center of the homepage is a picture of Jack and Rexella looking no older than they were when I watched them twenty years ago. But now they were sitting in front of a nice professional-looking faux news set.

I didn't have to search hard to find an episode to watch. A video player stands ready for visitors just under the featured image of Jack and Rexella. The date, July 28, 2018, let me know immediately they were still broadcasting their show. But when I clicked play, what I saw was incredibly jarring. For one, the set was different yet again. Gone was the polished, professional news set from the homepage. In its place was a simple television screen bearing the Jack Van Impe Ministries logo and hung on a wall that, though tasteful, would not have been out of place on a late-night cable access television show. Seated in front of the modest wall were the stalwarts of the program, Jack and Rexella. Rexella, always the ageless wonder, looked the same as she always has, much younger than her eighty-five years. Jack, however, was almost unrecognizable. If the name on the screen underneath the figure looking back at me didn't say "Jack Van Impe," I wouldn't have recognized him. His face was gaunt, clearly showing the wear of some terrible health battle that had taken whatever youthful vitality he had left. His eyes were sunken, framed by lines and bags that somehow made him look even older than eighty-eight. His glorious pompadour was gone, reduced to obviously thinning hair, slicked back in an effort to keep up the illusion of beauty.[1]

Listening to him talk was painful. Watching him in high school, I marveled at how prophetic rants and biblical quotes rolled off his tongue with ease and surgical precision. Now he struggles to speak. Flashes of the old prophetic fire are still there, but they struggle to stay alight. A great part of the appeal of end-times theology is the veneer of strength and precision to its arguments, the almost scientific approach that makes it seem every bit as valid as the law of gravity. With that veneer gone, the apocalyptic magic has disappeared, revealing nothing more than an embittered and broken man rambling on about incoherent conspiracy theories.

I couldn't watch for long. As much as I now disagree with Jack, he still seems like an old friend. Seeing him like that is just too painful, too destructive to my illusions of a more innocent time. So instead of watching an episode, I decided to try to find out what happened to Jack, his show, and the apocalyptic world I used to love so much.

Where is Jack Van Impe now?

Until fairly recently, Jack and Rexella were doing okay. He had some health issues throughout the years, as anyone of his age would, but as of 2016 Jack and Rexella were still running a multimillion-dollar ministry.[2] But his fortunes had started to turn several years before that. In 2011, Jack and Rexella ended their years-long relationship with the Christian network TBN after a falling out between Jack and the network when Jack railed against Rick Warren and Robert Schuller on his show. He accused them of promoting "Chrislam," a fictional religion that was all the rage in right-wing media in the years following 9/11.[3] Driven by Islamophobia and a disdain for inclusivity, those who harangued this supposed religion believed that Christianity and Islam were being combined into one monolithic religion that would take over the world, usher in the end times, and . . . well, you can figure out the rest of the story. It's hard to say whether Chrislam was an invention of outlets like Fox News or folks like Jack Van Impe who are always in need of a prophetic foil. Either way, TBN wasn't on board with Jack calling Warren and Schuller out by name, and the two parted ways.

That wasn't the end of *Jack Van Impe Presents*, however. Jack and Rexella continued to independently broadcast their show for several more years, until a series of serious health problems forced Jack to take a leave of absence. The show continued for a while without him, as various guest hosts took turns stepping in for the prophetic stalwart. Eventually, Jack's doctors told him he had to stop broadcasting because of his health. His absence from the show resulted in what he claims was the loss of fifty thousand donors.[4] Without the revenue coming in from those donors, Jack says, he was forced off the air. But despite the budget loss and the warnings from his doctor, he was determined to continue his show, professing he was God's final prophet who had to preach the truth before the end, which is now very, very nigh.[5]

Without the financial support, Jack was left to broadcast his slimmed-down program on YouTube. The basic format is still the same. Rexella reads several handpicked, context-free headlines she finds terrifying and then turns to Jack to have him explain their prophetic significance. But the surgical precision of the old Jack Van Impe has given way to the sort of ranting you would expect of someone who watches too much Fox News. I'm sure the xenophobia and bigotry were alive and well when I watched him regularly. I was just on board with all of it, so I didn't notice it—or worse, if I did, I thought it the gospel. Either way, they are on full display now. *Jack Van Impe Presents* has become something of a cheap *InfoWars* knockoff, wrapped up in the language of biblical prophecy.

A once proud, articulate, vibrant preacher has been reduced to a broken, bitter, and angry curmudgeon who spends his days ranting about Muslims, Catholics, and anyone who isn't a straight white conservative fundamentalist, as well as about his health. *Jack Van Impe Presents* is a shell of its former self, and so is its host. It's a sad scene, but more sad is the type of person Jack Van Impe has become, and the way he uses the Bible to demonize and condemn anyone and everyone who doesn't look, think, talk, act, or believe exactly like him. Or maybe that's who he was all along and I was too blind to see it. In either case, it's painful to watch, not just because the luster is gone, but because I see so much of myself in Jack. Staring at my computer screen was like looking in a mirror. Staring back at me was not only the person I once was, but also the person I would have become if I had stayed on that path.

For all the superficial differences on screen and in his physical appearance, the Jack Van Impe I see on YouTube now is the same Jack Van Impe I watched so long ago. He is the living symbol of all the problems that end-times theology creates. He passionately believes he has been called by God to preach the truth to the world, but the "truth" he preaches is antichrist in countless ways—ways he simply can't see. His world is divided into the saved and the damned. As a result, all sorts of heinous attacks, language, and even violence become justified in the name of God and fulfilling biblical prophecy.

Watching Jack rant now, I thank God that I lost my faith in the rapture. End-times theology and its lust for vengeance, its celebration of wrath, and its burning desire to escape the world leads its followers to bitter and broken endings. If I had stayed on that path, I too may have become an angry old man who sees conspiracies around every corner, is consumed with a lust for vengeance, and is so obsessed with eternity he forgets how to live, love, and enjoy life in the here and now.

Down to the roots of American Christianity

But that's not just where end-times theology leads; it's where so much of American Christianity finds itself today. It is defined by what it opposes, by its hypocritical and Machiavellian support for antichrist leaders and policies, and by its baptism of hatefulness, ignorance, and xenophobia as "sincerely held religious belief." American Christianity doesn't just suffer from bad theology. It's lacking in love.

Now, you and I may reject those criticisms and say that we aren't like that, or the church we attend isn't like that.

But frankly, our opinion is irrelevant. If that's what the world outside the church sees, that's the reality we have to address: the perception that the kingdom of God is the realm of bigots, homophobes, hypocrites, and the willfully ignorant.

If we're going to change that perception (and the reality behind it) and be able to do the kingdom work we've been called to do, we have to first address the mentality and ideology that gave birth to the very real words and actions that fuel those criticisms. Rejecting the false teaching of the rapture and end-times theology is a start, but we have to go deeper. We have to go down deep to the roots of American Christianity, where an overly spiritualized, individualistic, self-centered understanding of salvation, heaven, and the Christian life dwells.

End-times theology didn't come out of nowhere. It wasn't created *ex nihilo*, nor did it spread like wildfire without fuel. It grew out of a version of Christianity that was radically focused on the individual, on how *I* can get saved, how *I* can escape this world, and how *I* can get to heaven. End-times theology is nothing more than the natural evolution of a form of Christianity that had already lost its moorings.

But a truly biblical, truly Christ-centered view of the end times can also be the very thing that rescues Christianity and helps us rediscover our first love. After all, Christianity itself was born in the fires of apocalyptic fervor. The early church and the writers of the New Testament believed fervently that they were living in the last days. Revelation wasn't written about a far-off future. It was written about how to prepare in the present for the imminent return of Jesus. Living as if we are in the last days can be the very thing that rescues Christianity from irrelevance and self-destruction.

If we see the last days not as a dark moment of fear and dread but as a moment of hope that was inaugurated with the resurrection of Jesus, then the end times become what the church originally understood them to be: a time of radical transformation, when the promises of God are made manifest in the here and now as the kingdom of God comes down to earth as it is in heaven.

I didn't understand it then, but I see now that my professor was right all those years ago. We are living in the last days, but not because the tribulation is set to begin and the Antichrist is about to be revealed. We live in the last days because on Easter morning, Jesus walked out of the tomb as the firstfruits, or beginning, of a new way of life. With Christ's resurrection, the old order of things began to pass away as all things are being made new, not just in some distant future, but here.

Now.

And we've been invited to participate in that redemptive work. That's what salvation is all about. It's not just about *me* not going to hell. It's the redemption and reconciliation of all of creation with its Creator. That's why we can and should talk about being left behind—not as a punishment for a lack of faith, but as a calling to use the power of the Holy Spirit to live out the promised kingdom of God here in the present.

We are the hands and feet of the resurrected Christ in the world, helping to usher the kingdom of God into a world in desperate need of the kind of healing, justice, liberation, and transformation promised in the book of Revelation. To be Christian is to live as if Jesus really meant what he said when he taught us to pray, "Thy kingdom come, thy will be done, on earth as it is in heaven." To be Christian is to turn that prayer into a way of life. To be Christian is to live as if these really are the last days promised by Jesus in which all things are being made new. To be Christian is to be filled with apocalyptic love and to live with an apocalyptic imagination that sees the powers of this world for what they are and resists those oppressive powers through acts of Christlike love for the least of these who are being trampled under the feet of the beast.

It is this sort of apocalyptic imagination that makes Paul not only an apostle but also an apocalyptic prophet. He wasn't spreading gloom and doom, and there is little of the mysterious imagery we typically associate with apocalyptic prophets, but Paul was an apocalyptic prophet in the truest sense of the word. He was someone who revealed the truth while calling the people of God to repentance and reconciliation with God. He recognized that in God choosing the lowly, God was turning the power structure of this world upside down, making the first last, setting the prisoner free, bringing justice to the oppressed, healing the sick, and giving new life to the dying.

But Paul didn't see that work as something that allowed Christians to sit idly by and passively watch God do everything alone. For Paul, it is "because of the impending crisis" (1 Corinthians 7:26), because "the time has grown short" (verse 29), and because "the present form of this world is passing away" (verse 31) that we must prepare ourselves for life in the new creation. We do that by transforming our lives into a living sacrament, so that like the eucharist, our sacrificial love for others enacts the promise of God's future in the present.

Nearly every page of every Pauline epistle is saturated with this expectation of the imminent return of Jesus. It's not wistful daydreaming about the future. It's practical advice for living in the here and now. Paul believed the present had a direct connection to the future he *knew* was imminent. Remember, those epistles of his are real letters to real churches; in them he gives real advice for how people in those churches should live their lives. It's all predicated on the idea that the return of Jesus is at hand and his followers should prepare accordingly.

But even though Paul fervently believed we would soon be caught up with Jesus in the twinkling of an eye, he didn't believe that was justification for checking out of this life. Rather, it was a call to double down on discipleship. Christ's imminent return was reason to incarnate the good news to as many as possible, because there wasn't much time left to do that before judgment was at hand.

But Paul understood something dispensationalists don't: God is deeply invested in this world, and the end doesn't change that. The Bible doesn't say the world will be destroyed at the end of all things. Paul says the *form* of this world is passing away, just as John declares that the first heaven and first earth will pass away. According to the Bible, the end of history is really just a new beginning, a renewal or restoration of the world we live in, not a total destruction after which God starts over from scratch. That's why salvation isn't the finish line but an invitation, why Jesus prays, "Thy kingdom come," and why heaven isn't the destination, but a way of life that comes down to earth in John's apocalypse. God is at work transforming this world and has invited us to participate in that restorative work until Jesus returns to bring that restoration to fruition. That's the truth revealed by the Apocalypse of John.

It's also the apocalyptic theology of Paul.

But what does that work look like? What does it mean to live in the last days if we're not deciphering prophetic signs or waiting for the rapture?

Agape for the apocalypse

How the followers of Jesus should live in the last days is exactly what Paul tried to flesh out in his epistles. The description of end-times living that Paul gave is—as we should expect it to be—directly connected to what Jesus said should be the foundation of our faith: love.

Remember that when asked to name the greatest of God's commandments, Jesus said that everything in the law and the prophets—that is, everything about faith—hangs on, or is shaped by, the call to love God and neighbor. Augustine echoed this calling by making it his rule for reading and understanding the Bible. In between Jesus and Augustine, Paul also used love as his rule for living the Christian life. But we often miss that, not just because of the reputation Paul has as a not particularly warm and fuzzy guy, but because the place he most eloquently and beautifully lays out his own love rule is too often misappropriated for romantic purposes.

The tradition of using 1 Corinthians 13 at a wedding reveals one of the fundamental problems of translating the ancient languages of the Bible into English. In English, we have one word for love: *love*. In the Koine Greek in which Paul wrote, however, there were four different words for love: *agape*, *eros*, *philia*, and *storge*. Each had a slightly different connotation. For example, *philia* is the sort of love that exists between friends or family. That's why the city of Philadelphia is called "the city of brotherly love." *Eros*, on the other hand, connotes the sexual sort of love found between two lovers. It's the word for love you would expect to find in a reading at weddings. But it's not the word Paul uses in 1 Corinthians 13.

He uses the word *agape*.

That doesn't mean reading 1 Corinthians 13 at weddings is inappropriate—not at all. But if we relegate 1 Corinthians *only* to the romantic setting of a wedding, we miss the apocalyptic nature of what Paul is describing. He's not talking about newly married couples. He's explaining how to live in the last days. That way of living is driven not by fear of the tribulation, anxiety about when the rapture will happen, lust for vengeance against our enemies, or Machiavellian ethics. It's shaped by love. By agape.

If you've grown up in the church, you've probably heard *agape* used at least a billion times to name countless different Bible studies, Sunday school classes, and churches. Still, it's worth taking a look at again. One translation of *agape* is "the love of God for humanity and humanity for God." It captures how God loves us and how we are to love God. In that way, agape is like the greatest commandment summed up in one word. If it is, then 1 Corinthians 13 becomes not just liturgy for a wedding, but a commentary on the greatest commandment and a guide for applying Augustine's hermeneutic to our reading and understanding of the Bible. And if all of that is true, then 1 Corinthians 13 isn't just a mushy, feel-good passage to read at weddings. It's our guide for living in the last days, a model of apocalyptic love.

That's the kind of love Paul is describing in 1 Corinthians 13: apocalyptic love. It's apocalyptic both because it's how we are to love one another in the last days and because it reveals the love of God. It's also the kind of love I had completely forgotten about in the apocalyptic fervor of my teenage years. I was obsessed with biblical prophecy but lacked love—the kind of person Paul warns about in 1 Corinthians 13. It wasn't that Paul was opposed to prophecy. Paul believed in prophecy—authentic biblical prophecy, the kind of prophecy that speaks the truth of God to God's people, calling us to a life of justice and service to the least of these. That kind of prophecy is found throughout the surrounding chapters in his letter to the Corinthians. But even if we embrace the future-telling elements of biblical prophecy, even if we go even further and fully embrace dispensationalism—even then the kind of prophecy and code-breaking celebrated by end-times theology is of little value to Paul if it's not driven by love.

As he writes in 1 Corinthians, "If I speak in the tongues of mortals and of angels, but do not have love, I am a noisy gong or a clanging cymbal. And if I have prophetic powers, and understand all mysteries and all knowledge, and if I have all faith, so as to remove mountains, but do not have love, I am nothing" (1 Corinthians 13:1-2).

This would be a poignant passage in any context, but it becomes even more poignant in the context of end-times theology, with its army of experts dissecting and bloviating about every Bible verse and news headline as if they've got everything figured out and anyone who doesn't accept their teaching is either a fool or an enemy. I'm not just talking about Jack Van Impe or Tim LaHaye here. I'm talking about me. For all the damage that dispensationalist television and book experts do to the theology of the church, it's their disciples—arrogant, condescending, combative, sanctified, hateful people like me—who do far more damage to the witness of the church. Jack Van Impe and Tim LaHaye spread their theology across the airwaves and the pages of books to the masses. Then people like me put it into action, attacking people face-to-face, shaming them for their ignorance, and condemning them for whatever sin we think they are guilty of.

I had no love in my life, only wrath. For all my faux expertise and righteous conviction that I was on a mission from God, I was nothing more than a resounding gong, a clanging cymbal, an obnoxious guarantee that anyone who saw how I treated others would not want anything to do with Jesus.

I was also a child, both literally and metaphorically. As Paul said, "I talked like a child, I thought like a child, I reasoned like a child" (1 Corinthians 13:11 NIV). My childhood, or at least my adolescence, was driven by childish thinking. Of course, there's nothing abnormal about that. We all think like children when we're kids. The problem I had was thinking that, as a child, I already had it all figured out. I was the very thing Paul warned about. I believed I had the gift of understanding prophecy and that I could fathom all the mysteries and knowledge of the end times. I knew beyond any shred of doubt that my faith could move mountains. But love? I never really gave it much thought. I had too much else on the brain, too much else to think about to worry about love.

As great a Christian as I thought I had become, as hard as I tried to be perfect and never miss church, always read my Bible, always pray, never drink, never swear, and always call sinners to account, in my quest to not be left behind, I had forgotten my first love.

I had forgotten why I became a Christian in the first place.

I had forsaken the lessons I learned as a child in Grandma Ruthie's Sunday school class. I had forgotten that what drew me to Christ in the first place wasn't a fear of hell, but the love of Jesus that Grandma Ruthie displayed so selflessly for me, for everyone else in that class, and for everyone else she ever taught or came into contact with.

I forgot that that's what salvation looks like: God's love made manifest in our lives, giving us new life so that we can turn around and share that love with others as all of creation is brought back into a loving relationship with its Creator.

When I was a child I talked like a child; I thought like a child; I reasoned like a child. And like a child, I made the world all about me. I'm an adult now, and I wish I could join with Paul to say with confidence that I've put the ways of childhood behind me. But that wouldn't be true. I still struggle with humility, with the need to be right, with dehumanizing my enemies, with all the things I thought I gave up when I left the rapture behind.

My sin is the same sin Jesus called the church in Ephesus to account for in the second chapter of Revelation. They did the things they were supposed to do: refused to tolerate wicked people, tested the theology of their leaders, and persevered through persecution. But they had forgotten how to love.

Remember the love

It's curious that a lack of love in the last days is the thing Jesus calls out the church in Ephesus for. It's curious because it was in Ephesus that Paul likely wrote his first letter to the church in Corinth—the letter containing his now-famous description of love. Maybe it was that lost love that Paul saw and that inspired his words to the church in Corinth. It's curious, but not necessarily surprising. There's nothing unique about forgetting or forsaking our first love. If anything, it's something of a perverse Christian tradition. If nothing else, the story of the church is the story of people who struggle to remember the love that gave birth to our faith. And in our forgetfulness we replace that love with dogmatism, legalism, and oppression.

It's a tale as old as the faith itself, and one that continues to be told today. We've forsaken our first love. Oh sure, we talk about love a lot, preach sermons about it, write books about it, and plaster it on T-shirts, mugs, and wall décor. But we've forgotten that love is more than just an idea, more than an emotion, more than something that makes us feel good. We've forgotten that for Christians, love is a way of life. If God is love and we are made in the image of God, then we are made to love. It's why Jesus said the greatest commandment is love. It's the defining mark of our identity not just as Christians but as human beings.

But for too long we've kept that love to ourselves, sharing it only with people we deem worthy, people who already love us back. We love only those who love us back, and expect a reward for something even the pagans do (Luke 6:32). We've forgotten that our first love is Jesus, love made flesh. There was no one unworthy of his love, no one unworthy of his acts of mercy, healing, feeding, forgiveness, grace, inclusion, and sacrifice.

However, even if we do rediscover the apocalyptic call to love and serve the least of these, we must make sure to keep our focus on loving them as an end in itself rather than turning them into just another checkmark in our pursuit of heaven. We have to make sure we don't objectify them as charity cases or potential converts. Rather, we must love them fully and simply, just as we would any other person in our lives. For as Paul warns, "If I give all I possess to the poor and give over my body to hardship that I may boast, but do not have love, I gain nothing" (1 Corinthians 13:3 NIV).

It's only when we stop seeing people as potential converts, as potential jewels in our own heavenly crown, and start to

love them for who they are—loving them simply for the sake
of loving them—that we will begin to fulfill the promise of
Revelation. The apostle Paul tells us exactly what that kind
of apocalyptic love looks like, and it's the complete opposite
of dispensationalism.

Apocalyptic love is patient, kind, does not envy or boast.
It's not proud, but humble. It doesn't dishonor others. Dispensationalism proudly boasts about its secret knowledge and
condemns anyone who disagrees as the enemy damned to an
eternity in hell.

Apocalyptic love is not self-seeking or easily angered. It
keeps no record of wrongs and does not delight in evil. Dispensationalism is myopically focused on the self and fantasizes
over the destruction of its enemies for all the various ways
they've wronged the chosen few.

Apocalyptic love rejoices with the truth. Dispensationalism
rejoices in hearing whatever its tickling ears need to hear to
confirm that its adherents are right and the rest of the world
is wrong.

Apocalyptic love always protects, always trusts, always
hopes, always perseveres. Dispensationalism neglects the present, mistrusts its neighbor, raises fear about the future, and
looks to escape as soon as possible.

Apocalyptic love never fails. Dispensationalism always does.

Paul's choice of words at the end of 1 Corinthians 13 are
interesting. He says, "Now these three remain: faith, hope
and love. But the greatest of these is love" (verse 13 NIV).
Remain after what? Remain after putting his childish ways
behind him, after deciding to follow Jesus. He has given up
the legalism of the law, and what remains are his faith in Jesus,
his hope in Christ's return, and love, but the greatest of these

is love. As they should, the faithfulness embodied in the Law and the hope found in the Prophets hang on the greatest commandment to love God and neighbor.

The same is true for the Christian life. Faith in God is fueled by our love for God. Hope for Christ's return is driven by a loving desire to be with Christ. Love is the greatest of what remains as the old order passes away, because love is the animating spirit of the Christian life, the calling we've been called to incarnate, the bond that holds us all together.

But love is the greatest in another way too.

Love is the greatest thing we lack today. We talk about love, we preach about love, we even feel love for one another, but there's nothing particularly Christian about that kind of love. Christian love is defined by the love of Christ, and the love of Christ is defined by self-sacrifice, putting others before ourselves, transforming enemies into friends, and service to the least of these with no expectations or strings attached. But American Christianity is far too focused on the self, far too concerned with drawing lines in the sand between us and them, far too worried about being defiled by "sinners" to embody the radical, apocalyptic love of Jesus we've been left behind to share.

Jesus told his disciples to go and do likewise by loving and serving the least of these, but we've cuddled up to the empire, made an idol out of power, and gone out of our way to justify our allegiance to Rome. We've sold our sanctity for the illusion of power and privilege, comfort and safety. We've become the whore of Babylon that John tried to warn us about in his apocalypse, the one that sold its soul to the beast. We're the Nicolaitans whom Jesus warned about in Revelation, who confessed Jesus as their Lord and Savior but spiritualized their faith to the point of irrelevance, stripping it of its subversive power in order to make the Christian faith compatible with the Roman Empire. But we do more than just make it compatible. American Christianity doesn't just fit alongside the empire. In America, the empire is a Christian empire, a so-called "Christian nation." We've taken the mark of the beast and sanctified it in the pursuit of comfort and privilege.

But Jesus stands at the door and knocks. It's not too late to let him in and become the people he called us to be. It's not too late to join the ongoing work of salvation. Not too late to love and serve the least of these in these last days before Jesus separates the sheep from the goats. Not too late to stop worrying about the future and start caring about the present and the people in it.

Here lies the ultimate problem with end-times theology: it values prophecy more than people. Fulfilling biblical prophecy is more important than the lives of Palestinians, more important than those crushed by a foreign policy that's supposedly fulfilling prophecies, more important than those here at home who are forgotten and left to struggle because Jesus will make everything better one day.

Here, too, lies the fundamental problem facing the church today. We suffer from an idolatry of ideology and dogmatism. Even if we don't believe in the rapture, we too often love orthodoxy more than people. Being theologically right and keeping up the pretense of being right is more important than the lives and well-being of our neighbors. They may suffer, be oppressed, and end up ostracized by the people who are supposed to love them, but if our theology is right, if we're staying true to our ideology, we tell ourselves that none of that matters.

This is why, for all the distortions of dispensationalism, it's critical that we rediscover the apocalypse. Apocalypse, in its truest sense of an unveiling of reality, is the opposite of ideology.[6] Ideology is the tool the powerful use to control the powerless and to marginalize and silence dissent. Apocalypse reveals ideology for the empty power it really is. Apocalypse reveals the truth while empowering the poor and the powerless with a message of hope and the promise of divine action. That's why it, and not ideology, is good news for the poor. Ideology controls the poor and the powerless. Apocalypse liberates the oppressed, embraces the marginalized, sets the captive free, and gives life to the lost, the least, and the dying.

We miss this truth because our privilege blinds us to the needs that apocalypse promises to heal. Apocalypse promises hope for the poor and oppressed by promising to destroy the structures of power—structures that give us our privilege, security, and comfort. If we find that to be a terrifying message, it is because it threatens our status quo, threatens our place of privilege, threatens to take away our power and turn those we've always ignored and trampled underfoot into kings and queens in the kingdom of God. Apocalypse is only scary when privilege and power are being threatened. But to those Jesus came to serve, the apocalypse is the culmination of the good news promised to the poor and the least of these in the Gospels.

For the rest of us, apocalypse is a call to repent and an invitation to participate in God's liberating, justice-restoring work in the world. Apocalypse isn't a call to figure out secret codes that will unlock a prophetic map to the future. Apocalypse calls us to be vigilant of the signs, but only so that we will be ready to stand up to the false prophets at work in the world, name them for what they are, and resist, not through acts of violence, but through Christlike love for our enemies and service to our neighbors.

This is how we work out our salvation in the last days.

Resisters and liberators

As a kid, I sometimes heard the Bible described as a training manual. The people who described it to me that way meant it in the sense of a book that would help me learn what sins not to commit. It sounds hokey to me now, but the training manual metaphor wasn't completely wrong. The Bible *does* train us. It trains us to be apocalyptic, to be resisters of the beast, to prophetically speak the truth, and to join in the liberating, transforming, and healing work of the resurrection. It's that resurrection power that is at the center of John's apocalypse, setting the stage not for some distant future but for the transforming work of the resurrection in the present. That's how the early church understood the resurrection, how Paul understood it, and how John understood it. Jesus had been raised from the dead, and because he had, the last days had begun. The salvation that began when he walked out of the tomb was being extended to every corner of creation. Not in some distant point in the future, but here and now.

That's why Revelation isn't a secret road map to the future. It's a guide for how to live in the present. As Paul puts it in Philippians 2, we work out our salvation by having the same mind as Christ, the same apocalyptic imagination that sees the world as it is and imagines what it can become through the power of the resurrection. Revelation is the culminating book of the Bible because it captures the biblical call to justice and imagines what the world will look like when that call is fulfilled. The new heaven and new earth promised at the end of Revelation is certainly a transcendent utopia, but that beautiful image is revealed to inspire us to live differently in the ugliness of now. Revelation isn't a chronology of what's to come; it's a way of thinking about the transforming power of the resurrection and how it can be lived now.

But as we begin to develop our apocalyptic imaginations, we must not forget the communal nature of that call or else we'll stay mired in the individualism and overspiritualization that has plagued American Christianity for so long. We are saved together, and we are invited to usher in the kingdom of God on earth as it is in heaven together. Salvation is communal and so is the apocalypse. It's something that happens to and through all of us. We live out the future in the present together. We incarnate the vision of Revelation the way we practice the sacraments. We do it together as a present act that professes and incarnates a future hope already beginning to be realized in the here and now.

One of the things readers say they love most about the Left Behind series is the way it brings the Bible to life. Of course, it brought LaHaye and Jenkins's dispensational fantasies, not the Bible, to life. But there is a call or complaint there that we shouldn't miss. We *should* be bringing the Bible to life! If the flawed theology of dispensationalism has been able to do that, it's only because we've failed to bring the real promise of Revelation to life. As the prophet John put it, we've taken away words from his prophecy (Revelation 22:19). Not in the literal sense of editing them out, but in the deeper, spiritual sense of ignoring our calling and failing to live out the good news of the gospel. We've been merely hearers of the word and not doers (James 1:22).

If the church is going to have any relevance in an increasingly post-Christian world, it won't be through more programming or better worship-entertainment, and it certainly won't be through cozying up to the empire. It will be by rediscovering our apocalyptic imagination and learning to love the lost, the least, and the dying. But what does that look like in a tangible, practical way? What does apocalyptic love look like when put into practice?

The answer is found in Revelation and its call to resistance—a call to resist the temptation of the beast, the lies of the false prophet, and the seduction of Babylon's power. It's not the violent resistance of taking up arms so graphically represented in the Left Behind series. It's the subversive, nonviolent resistance of Christlike discipleship that's shaped and defined by love. Not just any love, but the kind of enemy-loving, other-welcoming, justice-giving apocalyptic love described by Paul and lived out by Jesus. This kind of love conquers the beast not as a roaring lion, but as a slaughtered lamb. This kind of love has power found not in oppression and conquest but in humility, servitude, and death to self.

It's the kind of love found in the apocalypse of Matthew 25 that loves and cares for the least of these.

It's the kind of love that drives out fear to welcome refugees from war-torn lands. It's the kind of love that mourns for the plight of desperate immigrants fleeing poverty and violence by making them our neighbors instead of criminals. It's the kind of love that doesn't blame the poor for being poor but instead makes their welfare our burden to carry. It's the kind of love that cares for the sick regardless of their ability to pay, the kind of love that feeds the hungry and quenches the thirst of the thirsty regardless of who they are, where they come from, what they've done, why they hunger or thirst, or what they'll do afterward. It's the kind of love that clothes the nakcd just as God clothed us in the garden. It's the kind of love that sees prisoners as people in need of redemption instead of villains without hope. It's the kind of love that welcomes the Other, whether they be people of other faiths, other genders, other sexualities, other countries, other languages, or other races, and welcomes them with open arms, making a space for them at the table and treating them as equal bearers of the image of God.

It's the kind of love that declares the truth of Revelation by living it out in the present.

The kind of love that inspires a faith worth believing in.

The kind of love that builds a church worth belonging to.

The kind of love that reveals a Jesus worth following.

Acknowledgments

I don't know how you go about saying thank you to everyone who has had an impact on a book that has been a lifetime in the making. I do know that I will forget people I should not have forgotten, so before I thank anyone, I want to first offer my apologies to anyone I unintentionally leave out.

Now, on with the show.

To Kim: you never cease to amaze me each and every day. Seriously, I will never get over the fact that you cut people open for a living. You're an amazing doctor and an even more incredible mother. Thank you for being my sounding board, my muse, my rock, my fellow traveler, my wife, and most of all, thank you for finally developing a taste for Chick-fil-A.

To Ainsley and Eleanor: before you were born I didn't think I could ever love someone as much as I love the two of you. Thank you for the gift of being your father. I can't wait to see the women you will grow up to be. Until then, please don't add this book to the collection of books you've taken off my bookshelves and torn to pieces. If you read it when you're older and decide to tear it up then, fair enough.

To my family, who taught me what it means to love, to learn, to believe, and to belong. And especially to my mom and my grandmother, whose faith showed me why women should never stay silent in the church.

To the Steves: my uncle Steve Pennington, who stepped in when my father stepped out and who helped ignite my creative imagination; and my mentor Steve Hoskins, for sticking with me even when my only goal in life was to see every movie ever made.

To Pete and Chad and Brian and Daren and Marvin and Nathan: thanks for putting up with an apocalyptic nut like me for so many years and allowing me the honor to count such incredible people as my lifelong friends.

To my in-laws: as I said in the book, you opened up my eyes to a whole new way of thinking about the faith, and that's great and all, but thank you most of all for just being normal. It's a really underappreciated quality in in-laws, and I can't begin to tell you how grateful I am for in-laws as kind and supportive as you.

To Matthew Paul Turner: I can't thank you enough for all of your kind words, support, encouragement, and advice over the years. This book wouldn't exist without your help.

To SFB: you've been there for me through thick and thin. Literally, I was a lot thinner before cancer and now I'm not so thin, but I'll never forget the love, kindness, and support you all have shown me over the years.

To Tony Sparrow: thank you for believing in me and showing me why youth ministry matters.

To the Calvos: I bet you didn't expect to see your names in here, did you? Thank you for being Jesus to me and my family when we were far from home and needed taking care of, even though you're both godless atheists.

To Rick Moore: thank you for teaching me that ministry is first and foremost about loving people. And just as importantly, thank you for teaching me how to find and appreciate good barbecue.

To Michael Pence: thank you for taking a chance on me and giving me my first full-time job in ministry.

To my friends, youth workers, and students at Covenant United Methodist Church: thanks for growing with me and teaching me more than I could ever teach you.

To Johnny Jeffords and Lora Jean Gowen: thank you for showing me the importance of justice and inclusion.

To Valerie Weaver-Zercher: thank you for believing in me. I hope I didn't let you down.

To my blog readers: I can't thank you enough. I know this is cliché to say, but this book really and truly would not exist without your support over the years, and for that I am eternally grateful.

And last, but not least, thank you to Dr. Pepper, for without the constant flow of your fine beverage into my veins, this book would never have been completed.

Notes

Chapter 1

1 Ann Byle, "LaHaye, Co-Author of Left Behind Series, Leaves a Lasting Impact," *Publishers Weekly*, July 27, 2016, www.publishersweekly.com/pw/by-topic/industry-news/ religion/article/71026-lahaye-co-author-of-left-behind-series-leaves-a-lasting-impact.html.

2 See, for example, the website aftertherapturepetcare.com.

Chapter 2

1 Timothy L. Smith, *Called unto Holiness*, vol. 1 (Kansas City, MO: Nazarene Publishing House, 1962), 114.

2 "Billy Graham's Life and Ministry By the Numbers," *Facts and Trends*, Lifeway, February 22, 2018, factsandtrends .net/2018/02/21/billy-grahams-life-ministry-by-the-numbers/.

Chapter 3

1 "About," Jack Van Impe Ministries, accessed October 10, 2018, www.jvim.com/about/.

2 Ibid.

3 I should add that although they are technically not always the same thing (since you can study or be interested in the theology of the end times without also subscribing to dispensationalism), colloquially, *end-times theology* and *dispensationalism* are often used interchangeably, and as such I will be using them interchangeably throughout the book.

Chapter 4

1 See Richard Kenneth Emmerson and E. Ann Matter, "The Apocalypse in Early Medieval Exegesis," in *The Apocalypse in the Middle Ages* (Ithaca, NY: Cornell University Press, 1993), 43.

2 Barbara Rossing, *The Rapture Exposed: The Message of Hope in the Book of Revelation* (New York: Basic Books, 2005), 22.

3 Jason Boyett, *Pocket Guide to the Apocalypse: The Official Field Manual for the End of the World* (Orlando: Relevant Books, 2005), 35.

4 Ibid., 39.

5 Ibid., 40.

6 Ibid., 41.

7 Ibid., 55.

8 Ibid., 67.

9 See Zack Hunt, "May 21st—An Interview with the People behind the Campaign!!!" *Zack Hunt*, May 10, 2011, http://www.patheos.com/blogs/zackhunt/2011/05/may-21st-an-interview-with-the-people-behind-the-campaign/.

Chapter 5

1 See Paul Ricœur, *The Symbolism of Evil* (Boston: Beacon Press, 1967).

2 Bob Allen, "Southern Baptists Have Lost a Million Members in 10 Years," Baptist News Global, June 9, 2017, https://baptistnews.com/article/southern-baptists-lost-million-members-10-years/.

3 Anne Lamott, *Plan B: Further Thoughts on Faith* (New York: Riverhead Books, 2006), 256–57.

Chapter 6

1 Barbara Rossing, *The Rapture Exposed: The Message of Hope in the Book of Revelation* (New York: Basic Books, 2005), 176.

2 Ibid., 178.

3 Chris Mitchell, "'I See Us in the Middle of Prophecy!' Mike Evans Has 30M Evangelicals Praying for Jerusalem," Christian Broadcasting Network, December 10, 2017, www1.cbn.com/cbnnews/israel/2017/december/mike-evans-we-rsquo-re-in-the-middle-of-prophecy.

4 Rossing, *The Rapture Exposed*, 45.

5 David M. Halbfinger, Isabel Kershner, and Declan Walsh, "Israel Kills Dozens at Gaza Border as U.S. Embassy Opens in Jerusalem," *New York Times*, May 14, 2018, www.nytimes.com/2018/05/14/world/middleeast/gaza-protests-palestinians-us-embassy.html.

6 Robert P. Jones, "White Evangelical Support for Donald Trump at All-Time High," PRRI, April 18, 2018, https://www.prri.org/spotlight/white-evangelical-support-for-donald-trump-at-all-time-high/.

7 Tara Isabella Burton, "The Biblical Story the Christian Right Uses to Defend Trump," Vox, March 5, 2018, www.vox.com/identities/2018/3/5/16796892/trump-cyrus-christian-right-bible-cbn-evangelical-propaganda.

8 See, for example, "Climate Change: How Do We Know?"
NASA, last modified October 3, 2018, https://climate.nasa
.gov/evidence/.

Chapter 7

1 In an ironic or perhaps inevitable twist of fate (since the
Christian writing world is relatively small), Jason and I met
years later and have since become friends.

2 Barbara Rossing, *The Rapture Exposed: The Message of
Hope in the Book of Revelation* (New York: Basic Books,
2005), 98.

3 Origen, *De Principiis*, in vol. 4 of *The Ante-Nicene Fathers:
Translations of the Writings of the Fathers down to A.D.
325*, ed. Alexander Roberts and James Donaldson (Buffalo,
NY: Christian Literature Publishing, 1885), 373.

4 See Saint Augustine of Hippo, *The Literal Meaning of
Genesis*, trans. and anno. John Hammond Taylor, Ancient
Christian Writers 41 (New York: Newman Press, 1982).

5 Saint Augustine, *On Christian Doctrine*, trans. J. F. Shaw,
in vol. 2 of *A Select Library of the Nicene and Post-Nicene
Fathers of the Christian Church*, ed. Philip Schaff (New
York: Charles Scribner's Sons, 1887), 533.

6 Origen, *De Principiis*, 364.

Chapter 8

1 John J. Collins, *The Apocalyptic Imagination: An Introduction to Jewish Apocalyptic Literature* (Grand Rapids:
William B. Eerdmans Publishing Company, 1998), 256.

2 Pablo Richard, *Apocalypse: A People's Commentary on the
Book of Revelation*, 2nd ed. (Maryknoll, New York: Orbis
Books, 1995), 34.

3 Barbara Rossing, *The Rapture Exposed: The Message of
Hope in the Book of Revelation* (New York: Basic Books,
2005), 117.

4 Richard, *Apocalypse: A People's Commentary*, 30.

5 Walter Brueggemann, *Prophetic Imagination* (Minneapolis: Augsburg Fortress, 2001), 36.

6 Ibid.

7 Shelia M. Poole, "Why Evangelicals Still Line up behind Trump after Child Separations," *Atlanta Journal-Constitution*, June 21, 2018, www.ajc.com/lifestyles/religion/why-evangelicals-still-line-behind-trump-after-child-separations/RAcnilDoh1OCDU7LbT9TrL/.

8 Rossing, *The Rapture Exposed*, 127.

9 Richard, *Apocalypse: A People's Commentary*, 86.

10 Collins, *The Apocalyptic Imagination*, 264.

Chapter 9

1 "Tony Campolo," YouTube video, 9:09, from *The Hour*, posted by "Strombo," April 2, 2007, www.youtube.com/watch?v=m584z5aE4Uc.

2 See, for example, Richard B. Hays, *The Faith of Jesus Christ: The Narrative Substructure of Galatians 3:1–4:11* (Grand Rapids, MI: Eerdmans, 2002).

3 Theodore Stylianopoulos, "I Know Your Works," *Apocalyptic Thought in Early Christianity*, ed. Robert J. Daly (Ada, Michigan: Baker Academic, 2009), 18–19.

4 Barbara Rossing, *The Rapture Exposed: The Message of Hope in the Book of Revelation* (New York: Basic Books, 2005), 4.

5 Martin Luther King, "I've Been to the Mountaintop" (address), Bishop Charles Mason Temple, April 3, 1968, Memphis, TN, transcript and MP3 audio, 43:11, https://kinginstitute.stanford.edu/king-papers/documents/ive-been-mountaintop-address-delivered-bishop-charles-mason-temple.

Chapter 10

1 Since writing this in the summer of 2018, Jack and Rexella have once again revamped their set to resemble the more polished look it had previously. Jack himself also appears to be in better health.

2 "Jack Van Impe Ministries International," Charity Navigator, last modified February 1, 2018, www.charitynavigator .org/index.cfm?bay=search.summary&orgid=3913.

3 Adelle M. Banks, "'Chrislam' Comments Force Christian Broadcaster Off-Air," *Huffington Post*, August 20, 2011, www.huffingtonpost.com/entry/van-impe-rick-warren-robert-schuller_n_880741.

4 "Jack Van Impe Presents—June 9, 2018," YouTube video, 45:32, Jack Van Impe Ministries, June 8, 2018, www .youtube.com/watch?v=Aez_u7AtHYE.

5 Ibid.

6 Pablo Richard, *Apocalypse: A People's Commentary on the Book of Revelation* (Maryknoll, New York: Orbis Books, 1998), 26.

The Author

Zack Hunt is a popular blogger, writer, and ordained elder in the Church of the Nazarene. His writing on faith and politics has appeared in *Huffington Post*, *Relevant Magazine*, *Patheos*, and *Youth Worker Journal*. He has also made cameo appearances in places like *The Boston Globe* and *New York Magazine*. After spending nearly a decade in youth ministry, Zack attended Yale Divinity School, where he graduated with a master's degree in Christian history. He and his wife and two daughters live in Tennessee where he spends his free time trying to smoke the perfect rack of ribs on his beloved Weber grill.